PRAISE FOR *OLIVER*

"*Oliver* is a love story of the most extraordinary kind. A man's frantic journey to find his best friend in the world leads him on a soul-searching trek to find himself through forgiveness and love. It's a story about feeling alone for so long, and then suddenly being connected to everyone. You'll need some alone time for this read, and tissues—it's a deep dive into our own hearts. And it's what the world needs now."

—GENEVIEVE PITURRO, AUTHOR OF *PURPOSE, PASSION, AND PAJAMAS* AND FOUNDER OF PAJAMA PROGRAM

"As a dog lover and psychologist, I consistently witness the remarkable healing power of the unconditional love and companionability of wet noses and wagging tails. When all seems lost, dogs provide emotional support, stability, and hope. Steven Carino's tender book is much more than a book about a stolen dog. It is about loss, despair, kindheartedness, friendship, and community. Steven and Oliver were inseparable; traveling companions through life. When Oliver is stolen, Steven is in crisis; forced to confront his beliefs about himself, his family, his relationship with others, and most challenging of all, with God (dog spelled backwards). *Oliver* is a story of loyalty, perseverance, transformation and renewal. Steven, with the consistent encouragement and ingenuity of his sisters, friends, and strangers, takes a journey to find his dog and unexpectedly, through compassion and empathy, finds himself."

—DALE V. ATKINS, PhD, PSYCHOLOGIST, MEDIA COMMENTATOR, AND COAUTHOR OF *THE KINDNESS ADVANTAGE*

"A lovely and inspiring story of how a community helped a man reunite with his very special soulmate, Oliver, and how their experience transformed the two of them. This book is a definite heartwarmer."

—CLAUDIA KAWCZYNSKA, EDITOR-IN-CHIEF AT *THE BARK*

OLIVER

the
True Story
of a **Stolen Dog**
and the **Humans**
He Brought
Together

STEVEN J. CARINO

AND ALEX TRESNIOWSKI

NELSON
BOOKS

An Imprint of Thomas Nelson

Oliver

Published in Nashville, Tennessee, by Nelson Books, an imprint of Thomas Nelson. Nelson Books and Thomas Nelson are registered trademarks of HarperCollins Christian Publishing, Inc.

Thomas Nelson titles may be purchased in bulk for educational, business, fundraising, or sales promotional use. For information, please email SpecialMarkets@ ThomasNelson.com.

Unless otherwise noted, scripture quotations taken from the Holy Bible, New International Version®, NIV®. Copyright © 1973, 1978, 1984, 2011 by Biblica, Inc.® Used by permission of Zondervan. All rights reserved worldwide. www.Zondervan.com. The "NIV" and "New International Version" are trademarks registered in the United States Patent and Trademark Office by Biblica, Inc.®

Scripture quotations marked NASB are taken from the New American Standard Bible®. Copyright © 1960, 1962, 1963, 1968, 1971, 1972, 1973, 1975, 1977, 1995 by The Lockman Foundation. Used by permission, www.Lockman.org.

Any internet addresses, phone numbers, or company or product information printed in this book are offered as a resource and are not intended in any way to be or to imply an endorsement by Thomas Nelson, nor does Thomas Nelson vouch for the existence, content, or services of these sites, phone numbers, companies, or products beyond the life of this book.

Unless otherwise noted, all photographs are from the author's personal collection and are used with permission.

Library of Congress Cataloging-in-Publication Data

Names: Carino, Steven J., author. | Tresniowski, Alex, author.
Title: Oliver: the true story of a stolen dog and the humans he brought together / Steven J. Carino and Alex Tresniowski.
Description: Nashville, TN : Nelson Books, an imprint of Thomas Nelson, [2020] | Summary: "The remarkable, life-changing true story of a lonely man, his lost dog, and the astonishing array of strangers who brought them back together"-- Provided by publisher.
Identifiers: LCCN 2020028547 (print) | LCCN 2020028548 (ebook) | ISBN 9781400223237 (paperback) | ISBN 9781400223275 (epub)
Subjects: LCSH: Lost dogs--United States--Anecdotes. | Dog owners--United States--Biography. | Human-animal relationships.
Classification: LCC SF427.6 .C37 2020(print) | LCC SF427.6(ebook) | DDC 636.70092/9--dc23
LC record available at https://lccn.loc.gov/2020028547
LC ebook record available at https://lccn.loc.gov/2020028548

Printed in the United States of America

21 22 23 24 25   LSC   10 9 8 7 6 5 4 3 2 1

To my mother, Marie Carino (1929–1976),
for always making me feel like your special boy.

To my father, Nunzie Carino (1921–1988),
for showing me the value of hard work.

To my brother, Frank Carino (1954–1995),
for teaching me all about the love of music.

Trust in the Lord with all your heart
and lean not on your own understanding;
in all your ways acknowledge him,
and he will make your paths straight.

—Proverbs 3:5–6 NASB

Contents

CONTENTS

Foreword

On June 2, 1963, I was waiting impatiently for my father's car to pull into the driveway of our home on Long Island. My sisters, Nancy and Annette, and my brother Frank were waiting with me. It was an exciting day for us, and down deep we were hoping the new addition to our family might make a difference—might make things better.

Three days earlier, we'd received word that our brother Steven had finally arrived. Our parents told us, over and over, that Steven was "a big boy, oh yes, a very big boy." I was twelve years old, and I took that literally. As I waited to finally get a look at him, I expected a giant baby.

My parents *meant* that Steven weighed nine pounds, eight ounces and was twenty-one inches long. When he finally came home, I could not believe how tiny he was. In an instant, I fell madly in love with my baby brother. I felt a deep and immediate bond to him. I attached myself to my mother's hip and helped her take care of Steven in any way I could. I couldn't get enough of him. Sometimes when Steven was sleeping, I'd sneak into my parent's bedroom and wake him up. Then I would scream, "Steven is crying. I'll get him!"

Over the years, our bond only grew stronger. Even as our lives went in different directions, we maintained our special bond. And we still make a point to see each other once or twice a week.

We share so many interests, and one of them is our mutual love of dogs. Steven's many dogs have always meant the world to him, as have mine. Neither of us has children, and we both think of our dogs as our babies. We think of them as our best friends—aside from each other, that is.

On February 12, 2019, two days before Valentine's Day, Steven and his dog, Oliver, came to my home for dinner. As usual, Steven and I sat in the kitchen and talked while Oliver sat in my dining room, barking. Steven called for Oliver to come, even though Steven knew he wouldn't—for some strange reason, Oliver was afraid of my dark kitchen floor. Steven tried to bribe him with treats, but it was no use. Oliver refused to budge. Oliver was afraid of a lot of things, and he particularly hated it when Steven or I raised our voices or there were loud sounds. He liked it when things were calm. I think it had to do with Oliver's charmed and peaceful life on a farm with his best buddy, Steven.

Two days later, my home phone rang a little after eleven o'clock at night. It was Steven. I knew he liked to stay up late, but he normally never called after ten. I immediately knew something was wrong, and Steven confirmed it.

Oliver was missing.

Oliver, the sweet little dog who'd helped lift Steven out of the lowest point in his life, who was Steven's best friend and brightest light, who brought Steven joy and love and purpose and sometimes even the resolve to go on, was the dog whose sudden disappearance, I feared, might break Steven's spirit and take away the funny, positive, caring brother I knew and cherished. Losing Steven was the last thing I ever wanted to happen, and even then, on the day Oliver vanished, I knew we might need a miracle to prevent it. But then, how often do miracles actually happen?

What follows is Steven's account of the incredible events that occurred after Oliver disappeared. I was with him for most of those events, just as I have been with him for many of the highs and lows of his life—just as he was always there for me too. In many ways I am still my mother's little helper, doing what I can to look after my baby brother. I wouldn't want it any other way.

As the story unfolds, you may recognize something I call invisible threads—the unbreakable bonds that connect human beings to one another, regardless of who they are or where they come from or what kinds of lives they lead. You may marvel at the power of community—of what incredible feats are possible when people come together in bad times. I hope you will see the love and gentleness and wonderful humanity of my brother, just as I do whenever we're together, and I hope you will learn something from his story, just as I did.

Finally, I hope the story of Steven and Oliver leads you to be extra thankful for your own invisible threads—the connections binding you to the people or pets who fill your heart with light and love.

—*Laura Schroff, author of the #1* New York Times
bestseller An Invisible Thread

Prologue

The first time we met—and maybe you'll say I imagined this—he looked at me as if he already knew me. What I mean is, he seemed happy to see me but not surprised. His manner was calm and knowing. He sat there with one ear sticking up and the other flopping down. And he tilted his head, as if he were thinking, *Oh, there you are. What took you so long?*

From the very beginning, I felt like we understood each other, as if we were hearing each other's thoughts—as if, somehow, we were able to communicate. For instance, beneath his eager expression that first day, I could have sworn he was thinking, *Hmm, look at this man standing here. This man here is sad. He is a sad human. I haven't seen a lot of faces, but I've seen enough faces to know that this is a sad face. But that's okay because he's here now, and I can get to work. I can do my job. I can start making him feel less sad.*

As for me, I was thinking, *Okay, this is my guy.*

Of course, I have no idea how dogs think. I'm sure it's not in complete grammatical sentences. More likely, they think things like, *Toy. Sleep. Itch. Kibble. Sky.* Nor can I say for sure they experience emotions the same way we do, though from research I know they are emotional, empathetic creatures. So, yes, it's possible I was imagining the connection I felt with him that first day, or I was projecting my own thoughts and feelings onto him, or I was reading something into the situation that wasn't there.

But I honestly don't think I was.

I'm also not saying that dogs can change our lives in an instant just by looking at us a certain way. Sure, dogs can make us smile, and they can lift our spirits—they have a whole bunch of tricks for that—but I'm talking about the big stuff. Can dogs change the way we feel *in our hearts*? Can they change the fundamental way we look at the world? Can they fix what is broken inside us? It's not easy to fix something that's been broken inside a person for a long time. So I'm not saying I believed that this one little fella could fix the thing that was broken inside of me.

At least not on day one.

But I did have the feeling—and I believe he did too—that of all the humans who could have walked into that particular store on that particular day, I was the human who was right for him, and he was the animal who was right for me. And once he knew that, I believe his little heart began to beat faster, just like my heart began to beat faster.

That's how, in only a few seconds, this dog took me from sad to a little less sad. He looked at me in his calm, knowing, familiar way, as if to say, *Well, here we are. We finally met. So come on. Let's go home. We belong to each other now. What are you waiting for?*

Valentine's Day
February 14

I believe he thinks my name is Stee. Not Steve or Steven, just Stee. You see, when he hears just the start of my name, the hard "st" sound, he reacts instantly, and the rest of my name becomes superfluous; the "v" sound never even registers. Or at least that's what I believe. So—I'm Stee.

As for him, his name is Oliver. Never Ollie, always Oliver. That's because it wasn't me who came up with the name. When I picked him up, I brought along the twelve-year-old daughter of the woman with whom I'd been in a long-term relationship. At first, she said she thought the dog looked like Chewbacca from Star Wars. I told her I didn't know what a Chewbacca was.

"Dad," she said impatiently, "you cannot let people know you don't know who Chewbacca is."

After studying his face for a while, she announced, "He looks like an Oliver. What do you think of the name Oliver?" Then she added: "Never Ollie. He's too sophisticated to be an Ollie. Always Oliver."

"Oliver. I like it," I told her. "It really works."

"Of course it works," she replied. "I'm really good at naming dogs."

Chapter One

It took me a while to understand it was real. To get that it wasn't a dream or a joke, that it was actually happening, and that it was happening to me. These moments of confusion may have been my brain's way of trying to protect me—blocking me from grasping an obvious reality. But my brain couldn't fool me forever. Soon enough, I understood. And that's when the nightmare began.

But let me go back to earlier that day, when the only nightmare I had to deal with was unusually heavy traffic.

I am a driver. I drive people from place to place in my small corner of the world. This is my job, and I do it well, and I like doing it. I like the tangible nature of driving—power and precision at my fingertips. I like meeting new people. If they feel like talking, I like hearing about their lives. I'm a pretty good listener, and people seem to sense that about me. Most of my passengers are happy to talk. Good conversation is part of the job.

I drive people to airports, hotels, office buildings, weddings, parties, sweet sixteens—anywhere they want to go. People call on me for college drop-offs and reunion pickups, for quick trips and long hauls. In the heated or air-conditioned comfort of my steel-gray 2015 GMC Yukon Denali SUV, over pretty much every stretch of asphalt or concrete in the tristate area, I bring people where they need to go. I know the Palisades Parkway and the Taconic State Parkway and the Merritt Parkway and the Sprain Brook Parkway and the Major Deegan Expressway about as well as I know my own driveway.

I also know traffic patterns, and I know ahead of time when and where I'll likely get stuck and for how long I'll be idling behind miles and miles of red brake lights. Noon on the Grand Central Parkway. Late afternoon on the Van Wyck Expressway. Pretty much anytime on the FDR Drive. I know that the density and duration of traffic are not mine to control, so I've learned how to handle the stress of it. I try not to take it personally when other drivers act in angry and dangerous ways. I'll admit that sometimes I get a little heated myself. But I know traffic can bring out the worst in people, so on most days, I try my best to adopt a very Zen approach.

On that day, it wasn't going well.

It had snowed that week, and snow always slows things down. I'd had to budget two hours for what normally would have been a seventy-five-minute trip, leaving my home in Bedford, New York, at 9:00 a.m. for an 11:00 a.m. pickup at the John F. Kennedy International Airport (JFK), forty-six miles away. I got there in time, but just barely.

The flight's arrival was delayed, so I had to sit and wait in a parking lot for two hours, which didn't much help my mood. Once I picked up my client and headed back to Westchester, the traffic was so intense it took me the better part of an hour to advance a grand total of two miles. *Two miles!* I didn't get back to my one-room, rented cottage until 3:00 p.m. This left me barely enough time to turn around and set out for my next job, a pickup in Katonah and a rush-hour drive into Midtown—the most hopelessly congested two square miles in the history of congestion and square miles.

On top of that, it was Valentine's Day.

Now, that shouldn't have mattered all that much because I didn't have a special valentine that year, and I hadn't had one for years—not since I'd split up with Gladys, but if I am being honest about our relationship, not even then. So it wasn't as if the traffic would force me to cancel a reservation at a pricey restaurant or be late for a home-cooked candlelight dinner. No one had much of a rooting interest in when I'd be done with my long day and finally make it home.

Well, not *no one*.

I thought about the long drive ahead and came up with an idea. I looked up the phone number of my next client, Mrs. Durant of Katonah, and tapped out a text message:

> Do you mind if I bring my dog, Oliver, with me for our drive? It's Valentine's Day, and he hasn't seen me all day. I promise you won't even know he's there.

I'm not the kind of guy who worries about what people think of me and my dog. I wasn't embarrassed about not wanting to leave Oliver alone on Valentine's Day. I happily admitted to anyone and everyone that Oliver was my best friend in the world. I know that so-called dog people will understand the depth of our connection, but others might not. Some people might think a fifty-five-year-old man who dotes on his dog and calls him his best friend and worries about leaving him alone on Valentine's Day is, well, a bit eccentric.

I know that. I just don't care.

From the moment we met, Oliver and I were a perfect fit. It's really that simple. Me, the garrulous guy with the New York accent, who doesn't tell a story so much as act it out with his whole body and who has a deep fondness for the gloriously svelte and vital Elvis Presley of 1956. And Oliver, the spiffy Yorkie–shih tzu mix, the rascally bundle of black and brown hair and big round eyes—so playful and so loving and so *good with people* and yet so sensitive to noise and disruption that he would hide under the dresser whenever I pulled the sheets off my bed.

Steven and Oliver. Oliver and Steven. Always together. Take 'em or leave 'em.

"Yes, of course. Bring Oliver along," Mrs. Durant responded.

I'd never taken Oliver with me on a job before. It wasn't the professional thing to do. But since my other little one, Mickey, had passed away in December, I was more hesitant to leave Oliver alone for long periods of time. So I was thrilled with Mrs. Durant's yes. Getting to take Oliver along on this trip felt like a serendipitous gift for us both.

"Come on, boy, we're going to the city!" I said as I opened my front door. Oliver jumped off the bed and barked and spun around and made it look like he understood we were going somewhere special—a trip to the big city!—when he would have been just as utterly overjoyed to accompany me to the end of the street and back.

Chapter Two

When I was four years old, I sat down with my mother and learned the names of all the US presidents. This was my first memory of being alive, or maybe my second, after the time I sat with my little red Show 'N Tell record player and stared in wonder at the 45-rpm record spinning around and producing this amazing sound. I can't be sure I remember the song that was playing—maybe "Java" by Al Hirt or "Barbara Ann" by The Beach Boys—but I definitely still remember all the presidents.

My mother would sit with me and teach me on the steps that led up to the kitchen in our house on Murdock Street in the town of Huntington Station in Long Island. She knew I had a good memory—when we watched the game show *Concentration* on TV together, she'd see how I sometimes beat the contestants at remembering which image was behind which tile, even at four years old. So she broke out our big encyclopedia—the volume with *P* for presidents—sat me down on the kitchen steps, and flipped through pictures of old men in ruffled white shirts with wild gray hair. One by one I learned their names in sequence—(1) George Washington, (2) John Adams, (3) Thomas Jefferson, on and on all the way to (36) Lyndon B. Johnson.

I remember as if it were yesterday.

Back then, people were amazed that a four-year-old boy could so expertly list the presidents in chronological order. It was seen as a sign of precociousness and potential. My father, Nunzie, who owned the Windmill Pub on Jericho Turnpike and also tended bar there, liked to bring me in, sit me on a barstool, and challenge customers to give me a number between one and thirty-six.

"Okay, thirteen," someone would say.

And I would reply, in my squeaky little boy's voice, "Millard Fillmore."

"How do I know he's right?" they'd ask.

My father would produce a giant *World Book Encyclopedia* he'd stashed under the bar for just such occasions.

"Give him another number."

"Twenty-nine."

"Warren G. Harding."

"Eight."

"Martin Van Buren."

"Thirty-three."

"Harry S. Truman."

Sometimes my father's brother would swing by and spend the day betting customers a dollar that the little mop-haired kid over there could name any president by number, and then he'd buy a round of drinks for everyone with all his winnings. I would munch on maraschino cherries, and my dad would give me a dime, and I'd play our favorite song, "Winchester Cathedral" by the New Vaudeville Band, on the jukebox. As the song played I would bask in the obvious pride my father and uncle had in me.

"You watch," my dad would say. "This kid is gonna be president someday."

My mother would tell me the same thing while we sat on the

steps and she taught me the presidents' names. "Steven, you could grow up to be president, too, just like they did." She said it to me all the time, and I believed her. I believed my father too. I began to think that maybe that was my destiny—to one day be president of the United States.

Many years later, when my life failed to unfold as I'd planned and I drank too much, lost my confidence, and found myself alone and living in a three-hundred-square-foot cottage on someone else's property, I still thought about what my parents had told me—that one day I could be president. Only now I wondered why they'd told me that; why it hadn't come to pass; who, if anyone, was to blame; and how this often-told story about my precocious younger self had become a mockery of the man I turned out to be.

In my darker moments, I thought about this silly prophecy and what it meant in the scheme of my life.

But that was only in my darker moments.

On Valentine's Day 2019, I wasn't all the way at rock bottom anymore. I had tentatively pulled myself up a notch or two. I had my job as a driver; I had my loyal, regular clients; and I had my beloved collection of 45-rpm records, which my father kept when the Windmill jukebox got refilled with new records, and then gave to me. I had my three older sisters, Annette, Laura, and Nancy, who loved me dearly and sometimes still treated me like the baby brother who needed watching over. I was, bit by bit, scratching my way back to something like an actual life.

The key to it all was Oliver.

The drive into Manhattan with Mrs. Durant was predictably grueling. The Henry Hudson Parkway wasn't that bad, but once I entered the city's grid, it was bumper to bumper. All the bicycle lanes stealing space from cars and creating choke points; all those Uber drivers flooding peak congestion areas and packing them even tighter. Driving in Manhattan had never been more of an endurance test, but as I well knew, there was nothing I could do about it, so why get all twisted up? I had Sam Cooke playing softly on the radio, and I was enjoying my conversation about music with Mrs. Durant.

And I had Oliver on my lap.

I got to Mrs. Durant's hotel on Sixth Avenue in Midtown. She was staying there overnight and taking a cab to JFK the next morning for an early flight. I helped her with her bags and arranged to pick her up at the airport in a few days' time. Then I got back in the SUV for the long, slow drive back to Bedford.

It was coming up on seven o'clock at night. I'd been driving for ten hours straight, and I was frazzled and hungry. Sometimes, at the end of a particularly stressful day, I like to sit beneath the Japanese maple tree outside my little cottage, light up a cigar, and feel the stress seep out of my body. If it's too cold to sit outside, I'll slide into the back seat of my 1972 aqua-blue Oldsmobile Cutlass, roll down the window, and smoke my cigar in there. I've never smoked cigarettes, and I'm not otherwise a smoker, but a cigar once or maybe twice a week—that, I enjoy. Especially on *one of those days*, which this day had certainly been.

I got on the Major Deegan Expressway, heading north out of New York City. I didn't have any cigars at home, and I knew my favorite tobacco shop, Ralph's Cigars in Scarsdale, wasn't too far away. I wondered if I should make the effort to get off the expressway and go to Ralph's or just keep driving straight home.

I was fifty-fifty about the cigar. On one hand, I pictured myself having a nice little dinner—pasta with olives and roasted peppers for me, a nice plate of Science Diet for Oliver—followed by a fine cigar in the brisk winter air, and that seemed like a pretty lovely reward for a long, hard day. On the other hand, I pictured a quick dinner followed by passing out in my bed and getting some much-needed sleep before the alarm sounded again at the unreasonable hour of 3:30 a.m. for my next job, a 4:00 a.m. run to JFK. That, too, seemed like a great reward.

Two things tipped the balance. One, the traffic was dying down. Getting off the expressway and on again wouldn't be that big of a deal. And two, surely Oliver needed to go to the bathroom. Oliver would wait if he had to—he was a good boy that way—but why make him wait? Why not get off at Central Park Avenue and let Oliver take advantage of the grassy border around the parking lot outside Ralph's, then slip in and buy a couple of cigars? What was an extra ten minutes after such a harrowing day?

I got off at Exit 5 and steered onto Route 100 North. I wound my way into the parking lot of one of the many strip malls built on the gently sloped hills along Central Park Avenue, where the town of Yonkers gives way to the southernmost edge of Scarsdale. Normally I'd pull in from the north, which put me on the upper level of the two-tiered, open mini-mall parking lot. But that evening, for the first time, I came in from the south and ended up on the lower level. The lot was crowded, but I found a spot. I shut off the engine, picked up Oliver, and took him to the stretch of grass overlooking busy Central Park Avenue. There was snow on the ground, but it was a peaceful spot, high above the noise of the cars, and Oliver was happy to get to trot around and feel the crisp winter air. He quickly took care of his business, and I picked him back up and put him in the SUV.

"I'll be right back. I'm just gonna run inside for a second," I told him. "You sit tight."

I locked the SUV with my key fob and hustled up the five concrete stairs to the upper parking level. A lot of couples were coming and going from the China Buffet, one of several businesses in the mini-mall, which also included a pet store, a hair salon, and a deli. *Of course,* I thought, *Valentine's Day.* Lovebirds out for a romantic meal. I smiled as I walked past them. I guess I'd been one of them, once. I skipped up another small flight of stairs and went into Ralph's Cigars.

I wasn't there long. I said hello to the owners, Ram and Sammy, and to the other guys who, like me, enjoyed hanging out there and talking shop. I remember pausing for a moment to watch the final puzzle on *Wheel of Fortune* before I picked two of my favorite cigars—Padróns, rolled in Nicaragua, about twenty dollars each—and paid for them at the register. All told, I was in Ralph's for probably four or five minutes.

Back in the parking lot, I dodged mounds of dirty snow and walked down to the second level. I unlocked the SUV and swung open the front door on the driver's side. That's when I noticed Oliver wasn't sitting up front, where I thought he would be, waiting for me.

"Oliver, come on up. Let's go," I said, tapping the center console with my fingers. "Come on, boy."

I glanced in the back and didn't see Oliver. It was a large vehicle, with three rows of seats and a cargo area set off by a small gate. Oliver had to be somewhere back there.

"Oliver, what are you doing? Are you gonna make me come back and find you? Come on, boy."

I opened the rear passenger door, expecting to see Oliver snuggled up on the floor behind the driver's seat. But he wasn't there. Had he wiggled under the seat? I reached down and poked around with my hand. Definitely not enough room under there for Oliver to be hiding. So where was he?

"Oliver, come on, now," I said, noticing the sudden change in my voice from normal to something hushed and lower, nearing a whisper.

I climbed into the back and searched the cargo area, where I kept my bartending equipment: two tables, a cooler, some boxes. Maybe Oliver had jumped over the gate and settled back there. He never had before, but maybe.

"Oliver, seriously, come on out," I said.

I couldn't find him. I got out and took a deep breath. *Okay, hold on, wait a minute,* I thought. *Think about it. Obviously, Oliver is in there somewhere.* I searched the SUV again, then got out again.

Okay, okay, wait a minute. Hold on just a minute. Of course Oliver is in there. Where else would he be?

I looked around the parking lot. People were still coming and going. I got on my knees and looked under the SUV and under other cars. I looked around the grassy area where Oliver had done his business. I didn't call out Oliver's name because it still seemed like a preposterous notion that Oliver had somehow gotten out of the car. Dogs can't open car doors. But, then, where was he? None of it made sense.

Suddenly I felt a sensation I could identify.

Panic.

And in that moment, I felt more alone in the world than I had ever felt before.

Slowly, I backed away from the car, as if it were booby-trapped. I heard myself say, "This is not happening." I slapped myself on the right cheek, fairly hard, and said, "Wake up!" Then another slap. I had to be sleeping. I *had* to be dreaming. But I knew I wasn't. My knees felt weak. I tipped forward and had to hold on to the car door to stop from crumpling to the ground. I heard myself breathing hard, and I felt my heart thumping in my chest.

"He's not here," I said. "Oliver's not here."

I ran through the parking lot and back to Ralph's Cigars. The man behind the register looked at me with shock.

"Oh my God, what's wrong with you?" he said. "You're white as a ghost."

"Did I bring my dog in here with me?" I asked. "Did I bring Oliver in? Did you see me with him?"

"No, no dog. Are you okay?"

I ran back outside. Now I was saying over and over, "Oliver, where are you? Oliver, where are you, boy?" My knees felt weak again, so I sat on the concrete steps connecting the upper and lower parking decks. I tried to control my breathing, and I forced myself to think logically.

Okay, Steven, go through the steps. He was with you in the SUV. You definitely brought him with you. You didn't leave him home and get all confused after a long day, right? And then you pulled in here and let him out in the grass and put him back in the SUV and locked the door and went into Ralph's, and when you came back he wasn't there, he just wasn't there, and . . .

Wait a minute.

Did you lock the door?

I'd bought the used SUV just two months earlier. It didn't feel new to me anymore, but neither did it feel familiar. For one thing, the key fob was strange. The buttons were in different places than I was accustomed to. Had I pressed the wrong button? Had I thought I was locking the door when, in fact, I might have been unlocking it? Was that what had happened? Could that have happened?

And if I *had* left the SUV unlocked, could it be that someone had come by and opened the door and . . . and . . .

I felt an awful, hard knot in my gut, like a punch—the mixture of shock and rage and vulnerability that comes with losing something that just a moment ago was there. The false, desperate hope that if you just look hard enough for it, the precious thing that was yours will still be yours because it belongs with you, right where you left it, and nowhere else. That the universe would not dare allow such a brutal disruption in the order of your life, in such a relative blink of an eye, for some unknowable, unfair reason.

And yet it was happening. It was real.

I took out my cell phone and called 911.

"Someone took my dog," I told the dispatcher. "Someone stole Oliver."

Chapter Three

The dispatcher asked me for details. Where I was now, where it happened, how it happened.

"I went into the cigar shop, and I came out and my dog is gone," I said, my voice unnaturally loud.

"How long were you in the store, sir?"

"I don't know, five minutes tops."

"Could the dog have run away?"

"No, he was in the SUV. The doors were closed! He couldn't have gotten out on his own."

I was yelling now.

"We'll send a car over, sir."

I looked at the phone in my hand. I noticed for the first time that I was trembling. I looked out over the cars and trucks cruising on Route 100 and thought of all the drivers heading home or to dinner or the gym, oblivious to the blessing of their uneventful drives. Five minutes ago, I had been one of them. Now I was someone else—someone I didn't yet know.

I would not be able to make my 4:00 a.m. job. Even then, standing alone in the snowy parking lot, I was clearheaded enough to know one thing: if I had indeed lost Oliver for good, I was finished. Finished as a normal, functioning man. Finished as someone with hopes and dreams for a better future. With everything I had gone through, to now have Oliver snatched away so cruelly would be, I believed, too much to overcome. This was not me being dramatic. It was the simple truth. Oliver meant that much to me. Without him, I would never be able to look at the world, or my future, or anything, the same way again.

And yet, I would have to keep on living in the world, and I knew there was only one thing that could possibly keep my mind off losing Oliver, and that was driving. Driving was my escape, my refuge. Out on the roads, I could keep my mind focused on routes and shortcuts and arrival times and conversations—anything except Oliver. Everything else in my life, I knew, would remind me of him. Everything. But driving—something I usually did alone—might not. So, within minutes of losing Oliver, I understood I didn't have the luxury of falling apart completely. I had to be responsible, to keep my job in case . . . in case Oliver didn't come back.

I called my early morning client, a regular named Renee. I told her what had happened and apologized and said I would help her arrange another ride. She told me how sorry she was and not to worry, that she would figure it out, and was there anything she could do to help? I thanked her and said I'd keep her posted.

"He's out there," I heard myself tell her, as if that fact was in my favor. "Oliver is out there somewhere."

That was as close as I could come to sounding a hopeful note.

I glanced around the parking lot. More happy couples leaving the China Buffet. I looked at my phone again. I already knew who I would call next. My sister Laura, whom I call Laurie—it had to be her. She was the organized one, the field general, the one who always had a plan. She wouldn't waste a minute worrying or even sympathizing;

she would get straight to work. She would know what to do and how to do it. And she lived just a few miles away in White Plains. Of course I had to call Laura and tell her what had happened. But I hesitated. I hesitated because I didn't want to call her.

Calling Laura would mean that it was real. It would mean that Oliver was really, truly gone.

Growing up, there were two constants in my life: my mother's unwavering love for her children and my father's drinking and rages.

My dad, Nunzie, was a good father. Sometimes a great father. He worked several jobs to provide for his family, and he built the house where we lived in Long Island from the ground up. He was funny and charming and adored by his clients at the bar and just about everyone he came across. He also dearly loved his children. I never doubted that.

But when my dad drank, everything changed. He became a different person. He withdrew into a hardened version of himself. He would come home and silently stalk through the living room, looking for a reason to blow up. When he found it—a misplaced toy, an imaginary slight—he would erupt in a rage. He might throw something across the room or break a piece of furniture. I knew this side of my father existed, even though he never turned his full wrath on me. I was the youngest, and I was spared much of what my four older siblings experienced. My mother, Marie, made sure of that.

My mother was fiercely protective of all her kids, but especially of me, her baby. I guess she had to be because I wasn't the most graceful of infants. At four months I fell out of my bassinet and fractured my skull, and at nine months I tumbled down a flight of stairs.

Thankfully, I sustained no major injuries, even when, at age six, I was hit by a van while holding two Mister Softee ice cream cones. Still, my mother felt the need to take special care of me. She also constantly praised me as a way to build my confidence. She brought me on trips to Manhattan, took me to my first baseball game at Shea Stadium, and, of course, taught me the presidents. In 1972 she somehow managed to persuade my skeptical father to buy me an organ so I could take lessons and learn to play it. I'm still not sure how she pulled that one off.

My life revolved around my mother. In some ways, I felt like I grew up an only child. My siblings were all significantly older than me, and by the time I was four and old enough to want to interact with them, they usually had better things to do than sit and play with me. The only things I could depend on were my records, my Matchbox cars, and my mother.

Which was fine with me. My mother meant everything to me. She was all I ever needed in the world.

And then my life changed forever.

I was ten years old when my mother sat me down and explained that she had been diagnosed with cancer. I didn't fully understand what that meant, but I knew from her voice, and from the heavy gloom that fell over our household, that it was very bad news. She battled it for three years, and when she went into the hospital for her third operation, I had a vague understanding that there was a chance she might not survive it, though no one explained it to me in those terms.

In fact, no one ever explained much of anything about our mother's illness to me. Part of it was to protect me. But part of it, I'm sure, was because it was just too wrenching a conversation to have with a young boy. Still, I knew what cancer was, and I knew how deadly it could be. I could see with my own eyes how my mother's health was deteriorating. I watched her make weekly trips to the hospital and come home with bottles and bottles of pain medicine. I saw her get physically weaker and thinner by the day. Nobody had to tell me anything.

My mother survived that third operation, and my sisters set up a comfortable reclining chair for her in the den. Still, she did not improve. She sat in the den all day, silently slipping away. One morning, my sister Laura, then twenty-five, led me outside to the front of the house. We sat next to each other on the curb, and Laura put her arm around me.

"Steven, Mom is really sick," she said. "We aren't sure she's going to live much longer. You need to get ready for that. We all do."

I nodded my head to show I understood. Then I stayed there on the curb and cried for a long time.

A black-and-white Chevrolet Tahoe marked "Greenburgh Police" pulled into the parking lot where I was waiting and stopped behind my car. No siren, no strobes—this wasn't that kind of emergency. A uniformed policeman, Officer MacGuire, tall, in his forties, stepped out and opened a small notebook. He asked me for my name and number.

"Take me through what happened," he said.

I told him the full story: long day, cigar store, five minutes, Oliver gone. The officer took notes.

"I don't mean to belittle what you're going through," he said, "but are you sure you had the dog in your car?"

"I understand why you have to ask," I said, "but, yes, I definitely had Oliver with me. Definitely."

"Did you lock the doors?"

"I thought I did, but that's the thing. Maybe I didn't. Maybe I thought I locked the car, but I didn't."

Officer MacGuire asked a few more questions and closed his notebook. He was being kind and thorough, and his face didn't betray that he was humoring me, but even so, I got the feeling the questions were a formality. How many dogs were reported lost or stolen every day? And how many of those reports ever led to finding the dog? *Probably not many*, I thought.

Later, I looked up the statistics. Each year, millions of household pets are lost or stolen. Many of those wind up in animal shelters, and of those, only 20 percent make it back to their owners. There's no telling what happens to the ones who don't end up in shelters.

The odds were not on my side.

"I'm going to look around the parking lot, ask around in the stores," Officer MacGuire said. "What are you going to do?"

"I don't know," I said.

"Are you all right?"

"Honestly? No. I'm in shock."

"Why don't you take some time to settle down before you get back in your car, okay?"

That was fine with me. I didn't want to go anywhere. I certainly didn't want to go home.

"I'm going to look around the parking lot too," I said. "I know I probably won't find him. But I'm going to look anyway."

"That's a good idea," he said. "If someone turns him in or takes him to the pound, we'll contact you right away."

I thanked Officer MacGuire and we shook hands. Oliver had now officially been stolen.

The parking lot was thinning out. It had been nearly full when

I pulled in; now it was half-empty. I walked around the perimeter, looking everywhere, poking at bushes, calling out Oliver's name. I realized I was going through the motions. No part of me expected to see Oliver in the shadows. One thought pushed its way past all others, much as I tried to fend it off: *I am never going to see Oliver again.*

I walked around the lot for a full hour. It was past ten o'clock at night, and the last diners were coming out of the China Buffet. Ralph's Cigars was getting ready to close. Only a handful of cars remained in the lot. I sat down on the sidewalk outside the row of stores. The night was getting colder, but I didn't care. I held my cell phone in my right hand and squeezed it hard. Finally I pulled up my contacts and made the call.

"Hi, Steven," Laura answered. "What's up?"

I couldn't find the words to respond.

"Hello? Steven? What's wrong? Are you all right?"

"Laurie, I'm fine," I managed to say.

"Is it Oliver?"

"Yes."

"Is he okay?"

"I don't know. He's gone."

"What do you mean 'he's gone'?"

"He's gone. I had him in the car, and I stopped to buy cigars, and I came out, and he's gone. Somebody stole him."

Laura asked more questions, including the question the police officer had asked—was I sure I'd had Oliver with me? Also, had I searched the SUV thoroughly enough? Could Oliver have somehow jumped out a window? Was there any other possible explanation?

"Laurie, Oliver is gone, and I don't know what to do," I finally said, my voice nearly strangled by despair.

"Stay right there," Laura said firmly. "I'm on my way."

I was still sitting on the curb when, twenty minutes later, Laura pulled her car into the parking lot.

It felt like the cavalry had arrived.

Chapter Four

Laura is the middle of my three older sisters. She's protective of me, as are all my sisters, but Laura and I are probably closer than any of the other siblings. Somehow we've always managed to live near each other well into adulthood, and we've often gotten together for dinner or just to let our dogs have a playdate. Laura is a dog lover too—something else we've always had in common.

The big difference between us is that I am a bit of a dreamer, scattered and messy, while Laura is driven and goal oriented. I've always been in awe of her ability to set a target, zero in on it, and blast through all obstacles to reach it. She's analytical, methodical, and fearless. I first saw that side of her during my childhood, when she mediated fights between our parents and defended our mother during the worst of our father's rages, desperately trying to bring order to chaos. She wasn't deterred by tough situations back then, and she's still that way today—a fact I was grateful for on the day Oliver disappeared.

I got up and met Laura on the lower level, near my SUV. She didn't say hello; she just got right to it.

"Let's search the car again," she said.

I didn't object, and together we inspected every inch of it, even the tiny nooks where Oliver couldn't possibly be.

"So, he's not here," Laura said.

"That's what I told you. Someone took him."

"And you looked around the parking lot?"

"For an hour. And the police officer did too."

"Okay," Laura said. "Do you think you're ready to drive home?"

I hadn't thought of leaving. It hadn't occurred to me. Leaving meant leaving without Oliver, and that didn't seem like an option. It made no sense at all.

"Yeah, I guess I am," I said.

"You're sleeping at my place tonight," she said.

"Okay, good."

I got in the SUV and followed Laura back to her home in White Plains, fifteen minutes away. It was the worst fifteen minutes of driving I'd ever had to endure. Halfway through I looked down at the empty passenger seat and noticed Oliver's favorite chew toy, a little yellow rubber duck, lying on the seat. I grabbed it and quickly threw it in the back. I felt so utterly miserable that I picked up my cell to call someone, just to hear another human voice. But it was late, and I didn't want to wake anyone up. The only person I knew for sure would still be up was my good friend from the fourth grade, Paul Perea, who lives in Missouri. I gave him a call.

"Paulie, I'm driving home right now but not with Oliver," I said. "Oliver was stolen."

"What? Are you serious? Oliver was stolen? By who?"

I told him I didn't know. I told him it had just happened. I told him I was afraid I'd never see Oliver again. Paul talked me through my panic and reassured me I would find Oliver—which was just what I needed to hear him say, whether he believed it or not.

"Stay strong, buddy," Paul told me.

For a moment I wondered if I should have stayed in the parking lot all night, just in case. Then I realized that would have been point-less. If I truly believed Oliver had somehow gotten out of the SUV on his own, I would have spent all night searching the surrounding streets and yards. But I didn't believe that. I may have left the doors unlocked, but I was sure I hadn't left them open. And I hadn't left a window open either. Oliver did not get out of the car on his own. Oliver wasn't lost. Someone had stolen him and taken him God knew where.

At Laura's charming, two-story, colonial-style home, nestled neatly on a street across from a country club, she offered me the upstairs guest room. I said I'd rather sleep on the sofa, where I usually slept whenever I crashed at her house. She brought down a pillow and some bedding. I plopped myself on the sofa and half sat, half lay there absently.

Laura's tiny brownish-gray poodle, Emma, no bigger than a shoebox, wandered into the living room. Emma had cataracts and couldn't see, but she had a system of sliding along the baseboards and softly bumping into walls with her nose, going from room to room, following the sound of humans talking. Normally I'd have been thrilled to see Emma, and I'd have scooped her up. Oliver would have been thrilled, too, and the dogs would have gone together to the backyard to bounce around and play.

But that night I couldn't bear to pick up Emma and hug her slender, precious frame to my chest. I wanted to, but I couldn't. Emma looked in my direction with her opaque eyes and curled up on the rug at the foot of the sofa, as if she knew something was wrong and she wanted to console me. Laura came downstairs, picked her up, and sat with her in a chair so we could talk.

We went over the details of the day. It felt good to have someone to talk to about Oliver. After a while, Laura suggested lighting a candle. It was something she did often, in memory of our mother, whose presence we both felt around us all the time.

"We'll keep the candle burning until we get Oliver back," Laura said. "I know Mom will help us find him."

Then she turned out the lights and went upstairs. I tucked in the white cotton fitted sheet, stretched out the top sheet, and lay sideways on the sofa, bringing my legs up nearly to my chest. Normally when I slept on Laura's sofa, Oliver would jump up, settle in the hollow between my arms and legs, and sleep there for as long as I did. Oliver didn't sleep in a dog bed. Whatever bed was my bed was also Oliver's bed.

That night, I struggled to keep my mind from churning through the events of the evening or, worse, playing out scenarios of where Oliver might be. At one point, as I drifted off to some version of sleep, I instinctively reached down to pet Oliver and was startled awake by his absence. This pattern repeated itself the whole night—short, fitful stretches of sleep ruined by cold bursts of realization. No matter what mental tricks I tried—remembering old New York Mets hitters, replaying World Series games, recalling lyrics from obscure fifties songs—I simply could not prevent the same torrent of terrible questions from flooding my brain.

Where is he? Is he barking? Is he crying? Is he chained up? Is he okay? Is he even alive?

Why isn't Oliver here with me?

The Search: Day One
February 15

Oliver is an introvert. Some dogs will greet the pizza delivery guy with a big sloppy kiss at the door, but that's not Oliver—Oliver doesn't make the first move in any relationship.

When I take Oliver on a walk and a passerby sees him and smiles and begins to talk to him—"Aw, such a cute pup. You're a good puppy, aren't you?"—Oliver always stays close to my leg and looks up at me. It's as if he's waiting for my opinion of this new person, asking, Is this okay? Is this cool? Can I trust this one? I'll nod and say, "Oliver, go ahead. You can say hi. It's okay." Only then will Oliver go over and wag his tail and let himself be pet on the head and otherwise be a perfectly friendly little dog. He's not scared of new people; he's just very thoughtful.

Which, I guess, is one of the reasons we get along so well—I'm an introvert too. I'm not immediately trusting either. In fact, Oliver and I help each other with new people. We embolden each other. We give each other permission to lay down our defenses and let the beautiful world in.

It's funny how dogs do that sometimes—bring out the best in you.

Chapter Five

The next morning, I awoke in the darkness of dawn with a terrible weariness in my bones and a feeling of such hollowness that I wasn't sure I could stand up.

Somehow I got to my feet and quietly shuffled through the kitchen. Laura was asleep upstairs, and I didn't want to wake her. I hoped she'd slept more than I had, which felt like not at all. I let myself out the back door and closed it gently behind me. Outside, the sky was only starting to let in little streaky slivers of pink light.

Instinctively, I went to my SUV in the driveway and searched it yet again. After a few minutes I got out and made a fist, punched the garage door, hard. I didn't even realize what I was doing. The next moment, I was down on the asphalt in a crumpled heap. Some of the shock of the previous night had worn off, and now the sadness felt intolerable.

This was the first day I had woken up without a dog with me in twenty-seven years.

More than anything, I felt a horrible, anguished sense of being alone. Of having no one and nothing. Of being cruelly and randomly abandoned by the universe. Abandoned by my guardian angels. Abandoned by God. And not just abandoned either—punished too.

For what, I didn't know. I remembered Proverbs 3:25–26, verses that stayed with me:

> Have no fear of sudden disaster
> > or of the ruin that overtakes the wicked,
> for the LORD will be at your side
> > and will keep your foot from being snared.

Well, where was Oliver now, in the face of this sudden disaster? My anger boiled over.

"How could you do this?" I yelled, looking up at the heavens. "How could you take my dog? I mean, my *dog*? The one thing I have in my life? What have I been doing these past forty years? Talking to you like you're really listening? Talking to my mom and dad like they're really listening? I must be an idiot! How could you take my dog?"

None of us really know how we will handle a crisis until we have to handle it. I always assumed that in such a situation, I would be calm and strong and proactive. Boy, was I mistaken. It turned out I reacted to losing Oliver by flailing in an ocean of self-pity. I am not going to pretend otherwise because I want to be completely honest in telling this story. And the honest truth is that I was a wreck. I was consumed by dread and resignation. Oliver was gone. He'd been gone for hours now. He was *long* gone. He could be anywhere, or nowhere at all.

So what was the point of looking for him? What was the point of life itself? I'm sure others would have reacted with less desperation to losing a pet, or at least not believed their lives were over. But Oliver wasn't a pet to me. Oliver *was* my life. Without him, nothing I could think of mattered, not even a little bit. I felt broken and useless.

What really frightened me, though, was that it wasn't like me to feel this defeated. I'd endured my share of setbacks, and I'd weathered them—not always gracefully, not always easily, but I'd made it through them more or less intact.

This felt different. This felt like a last straw. I understood what death was. I knew how to adapt to the death of a loved one. But in this case, I had no idea whether Oliver was alive or not. I was in the Twilight Zone. As a kid, I watched many of those old black-and-white episodes, with Rod Serling describing people caught in mystifying situations. Now I was caught in one myself. I felt like I wasn't dead, but I wasn't quite alive either. I was trapped somewhere in between.

After all, I had boiled my life down to the basics—a roof over my head, a decent job, and Oliver. I wasn't asking for or expecting much from the world. And yet the world had taken something irreplaceable from me.

I looked down and noticed that my knuckles were bleeding.

I tried to gather myself. I wiped my eyes and brushed the dirt off my pants and went back inside. I knew Laura would not want me feeling sorry for myself, not even for a moment. She's not heartless—she has a bigger heart than anyone I know—she's just determined. She had a long and successful career as an advertising sales executive, working mostly for the Time Inc. magazine empire, but she also helped launch *USA Today*, the country's first national newspaper, and she worked at *People*, the most popular magazine in the United States. She did it all without a college degree, without even attending college, through sheer willpower and determination.

Laura has simply always believed that hard work and dedication can make anything come true.

Sure enough, when she came down the stairs, she didn't waste a minute with small talk.

"Steven, we have to go back to the strip mall and put up some posters," she said straightaway.

"I don't want to talk about it," I answered.

"I know you don't want to, but you have to."

"Why do I have to?"

"Because we're going to get Oliver back."

"What?"

"I said, we are going to get Oliver back."

"How can you say that?" I asked. "He could be anywhere. He could be dead!"

Laura was as calm as if we were discussing a shopping list.

"We are going to get Oliver back because we *have* to get him back," she said. "It's as simple as that."

We both knew it was not that simple. But we also knew these were the words I needed to hear. We'd been here before, brother and sister, facing painful situations together. And together we had survived them. Now, somehow, we would have to do it again.

"Steven, please find a photo of Oliver for the poster," Laura instructed. "Make sure it's clear, and make sure it's really cute. We're going to put his picture *everywhere*."

In the fourth grade I kept my hair slicked down; wore gigantic, gold, wire-framed glasses; and carried my schoolbooks in a brown, fake-leather briefcase. I didn't realize all three of those things made me the biggest nerd in class. Most of the kids carried their books in their arms, but I loved my briefcase—it made me feel very official. So I walked around with it for the whole year.

One day during class, our teacher, Mr. Adams, was talking with students gathered around his desk. I walked by and overheard what they were talking about—US presidents.

Naturally, I sidled over.

"Was there ever a president who was elected and then lost, then got elected again?" one of the students asked.

"Yes, I think so," Mr. Adams said. "I can't think of his name offhand."

"Grover Cleveland," I announced.

The students turned to look at me standing there, somewhat smugly, with my big glasses and my briefcase.

"How do you know that?" one student asked.

"I just do," I said. "Grover Cleveland, the twenty-second and twenty-fourth president. In between was Benjamin Harrison."

Mr. Adams pulled out an encyclopedia and checked. Then he looked at me quizzically. He asked me what else I knew about Grover Cleveland. I said he was born in 1837 and died in 1908, and he served from 1885 to 1889 and again from 1893 to 1897. And he was a Democrat. Mr. Adams asked if I knew anything about any other presidents. I rattled off some facts about Andrew Jackson. He asked if I had a favorite president.

"Harry S. Truman," I said. "He's eighty-eight years old now, and I'm rooting for him to make it past the oldest ex-president, John Adams, who was ninety."

"How do you know all this?" Mr. Adams asked.

As proudly as I could, I said, "My mother taught me."

Mr. Adams looked at me with amazement. He was a big man with a crew cut, and he'd been wounded in World War II. Sometimes he walked with crutches; sometimes he used a wheelchair. Mr. Adams *loved* American history, and he challenged his students to memorize the Gettysburg Address. Every morning, he led us in saluting the flag. Not surprisingly, he got a big kick out of me knowing all the presidents, and eventually, like my father, he would walk down the hallway with me, stop other teachers, and tell them to "pick a number" between one and thirty-seven. I never let him down. This, of course, did not help my reputation as a nerd.

"You know," Mr. Adams told me that day, "you can write a letter to President Truman, and we can mail it to him."

I was astonished. I didn't know an ordinary person could write to a US president. Mr. Adams assured me that he would get the address, and Mr. Truman would receive the letter. That night, I sat down with my mother, and together we composed a short little note in which I told Mr. Truman that I knew the names of all the presidents, that he was my favorite president, and I hoped that one day I could be president too.

Less than one month later, my mother picked me up from my organ lesson with a funny little smile on her face.

"You have something special waiting at home," she said.

"What is it?"

"Oh, I don't know. A letter from President Truman."

My eyes nearly popped out of my head. We drove home, me urging my mom to go faster, and when we got there, I raced inside and snatched the letter off the kitchen table. I marveled at the elegant off-white envelope, which had Mr. Truman's big, bold signature across the date stamp, just above my name—*my name!*—Steven Carino.

When I opened it, I saw the letter wasn't actually written by President Truman; it was from his personal secretary, Rose A. Conway. But that hardly mattered. I figured Mr. Truman was a busy man. In fact, he was very sick at the time and would pass away just two months later. For me, it was more than enough to know he had read my letter and was encouraging me to keep up with my interest in US presidents. "History was his favorite subject," Ms. Conway explained to me in the letter, "and proved an invaluable help to him in his public life."

And finally: "Mr. Truman sends you his personal best wishes for a long, happy, and useful life."

I was blown away. My mother had the letter framed, and we hung it up on my bedroom wall. It was one of the best moments of my childhood and also one of my favorite memories of my mother. I could see on her face how very proud she was of me. It was a look I will never, ever forget.

There was one other time when my knowledge of the presidents paid off. It was the first day of eighth grade, and our social studies teacher, Ms. Neumeyer, was asking us questions about our new textbook. She asked one student where to look for the table of contents. She asked another where to find the glossary. Then she came to me.

"Mr. Carino, where would you look in the textbook to find out who the thirty-second president was?" Ms. Neumeyer asked.

My friend Mark was sitting behind me, and I heard him laugh and say, "Boy, did she pick the wrong kid for that one."

I was silent for a moment, so Ms. Neumeyer repeated the question. I looked straight at her and responded.

"I wouldn't have to look anywhere," I said.

"What do you mean?"

"Number thirty-two is Franklin Delano Roosevelt."

Ms. Neumeyer was puzzled. She asked if I had looked it up. I told her I hadn't. She asked me to name the twenty-seventh president, and

I said, "William Howard Taft." After that, Ms. Neumeyer moved on to the next student.

At the end of the school day, I raced home to tell my mother about it. She was very sick at the time, ravaged by her cancer, which she had been fighting for nearly three years. Her teeth had fallen out, and her bones nearly poked through her sallow skin. Her body looked impossibly frail. In her third and final operation, I later found out, the doctors had severed all the nerves in her neck, trying to alleviate her pain. They weren't even sure how she was still alive. Plus, all the medicine they gave her—Valium, methadone, some other injections—left her in a permanent fog. I was frightened by her skeletal appearance, but still I sat with her every minute I could, playing the organ for her, telling her jokes, stroking her hand, doing whatever I could to make her feel better. I knew she was suffering, and I knew that suffering would only end when she passed. But I didn't want her to go. I didn't want her to *ever* go.

That day after school I raced over to her recliner in the den, and I took her slender hand in mine.

"Mom, you're never going to believe what happened today at school!" I said.

My mother slowly turned to look at me, no trace of comprehension on her face. I continued anyway.

"Ms. Neumeyer asked me about the thirty-second president, and I told her it was FDR, and it was the funniest thing that I was able to name him without looking at the book. It was so cool!"

My mother kept her blank gaze fixed on me.

Then—she smiled.

It was a weak smile, not anything like her normal, beautiful, spirit-lifting smile, but it was enough for me to know that she understood what I was telling her and that she was proud of me, like she'd always been, like she always would be.

It was a beautiful moment. It was like coming full circle from where we started, on the kitchen steps, learning the presidents. I didn't fit in with other kids my age, even after I gave up my fake-leather briefcase, but I could always count on my mother to be there for me. She was my champion, my best friend. She was the whole world to me.

That moment with her, when I gently held her hand in mine, turned out to be the next to last meaningful interaction we'd ever have.

Chapter Six

I sat on Laura's sofa and dug through my cell phone, looking for a photo of Oliver. It wasn't easy. I had a million of them, but sifting through them—Oliver running in a field, Oliver in the passenger seat, so happy, so unsuspecting—made my heart ache. I finally found the photo I wanted: a shot of Oliver sitting in the grass and looking up at me, his face a picture of sweetness and innocence. I texted the photo to Laura, who was at her desk creating a flyer on her computer.

"Okay, so how much do you want to offer as a reward for finding Oliver?" she asked.

"I don't know," I said. "$2,500?"

That was just about everything I had in my account.

"Fine," Laura said. "Let's start with that. Now, we need a little story. We need to tell people what happened. Think of what you want to say."

Together, it took us thirty minutes to finish the flyer. "CASH REWARD," it read at the top in bold type. "$2,500. No Questions Asked." Beneath that was the story:

OLIVER, MY BELOVED DOG, WAS STOLEN OUT OF MY CAR ON VALENTINE'S DAY AT 1119 CENTRAL PARK AVENUE. I RAN INTO A STORE, AND WHEN I CAME BACK HE WAS GONE. IF YOU TOOK HIM, OR YOU KNOW ANYTHING ABOUT HIS WHEREABOUTS, I BEG YOU TO PLEASE RETURN HIM TO ME. WE MEAN THE WORLD TO EACH OTHER, AND I KNOW HE MUST BE TERRIFIED.

The flyer concluded with one last plea:

WE LOVE EACH OTHER VERY MUCH.
IF YOU KNOW ANYTHING ABOUT
MY SWEET BABY, PLEASE, PLEASE CALL ME.

Laura printed out fifty copies and slipped them into a plastic folder. The process of finding Oliver had begun.

Watching my sister operate so quickly and efficiently made me feel guilty. The whole search effort seemed pointless to me because, by then, I couldn't shake the idea that Oliver was gone for good. Even so, I didn't want to let Laura do everything while I sat there on her sofa sulking. I knew that sooner or later she would order me off the sofa anyway. So I thought I'd better contribute something.

As I sat there wondering how we could spread the word that Oliver was missing, I hit on an idea. Maybe we could get a local TV reporter to do a segment on Oliver. You know, one of those human-interest pieces they do every now and then. I found the phone number for News 12 in Westchester, the local station I watched, and I called them, but no one answered. Laura and I decided we would keep trying the station throughout the day.

Another plan formed in my mind. But it wasn't a plan to find Oliver. It was an escape plan.

If I had indeed lost Oliver for good, I wouldn't be able to live in the cottage anymore. I wouldn't be able to live in Bedford or, for that matter, Westchester County. It would be too painful. Instead, I decided, I'd pack a suitcase and leave. Just—leave. Go somewhere, anywhere. Maybe Florida. Get as far away as I could from my own life. The plan seemed so sound and logical to me that I suddenly blurted it out to Laura.

"You're not going anywhere," she responded matter-of-factly. "We are going to get Oliver back."

I wanted to argue with her, but I didn't. My misery was simply no match for Laura's resolve. But I knew in my heart that if I didn't find Oliver, I was going to disappear. Move away. And this time, I wouldn't listen to anyone's advice.

Before leaving that morning, Laura blew out the candle she'd lit for our mother. She only kept it lit when she was home. Then we got in her car and drove to my rented cottage in Bedford. I had to get a change of clothes, and I had to tell the owner of the cottage, Lucy, about Oliver.

Lucy was technically my landlady, but she was much more than that. She was my good friend. Together with her husband, Alan, Lucy owned a five-acre spread called Sunny Meadows Farm in the upscale hamlet of Bedford. They lived in the main house and rented out the one-room cottage just off the driveway. Lucy was a former high school social studies teacher and lifelong animal lover who raised goats and rabbits and chickens. She had an old, pure-white Welsh cross horse named Po (short for Pony Express) and a miniature cow named Anna Belle. Lucy also had a couple of cats, Willy and Georgie, who were in charge of the barn and patrolled for mice. Not long after she and Alan bought the property, they decided to rent out the hundred-year-old cottage, and they posted it on Craigslist.

That's where I found it. I'd just gone through a terrible breakup, and I needed a place to stay. I liked the rustic look and feel of Lucy's cottage, but there was a problem—the ad said no pets. Every rental property I looked at had the same rule. And I had two dogs then: Louie, my lovable Yorkie–shih tzu mix, and Mickey, my unflappable, apricot-colored poodle.

Still, something told me not to write off the Bedford cottage too quickly. I called the number in the ad, and Lucy picked up. I pleaded my case, but she firmly restated her no-pets policy. She didn't want a dog on the property interfering with her cats and their barn watching and mouse patrolling.

"Okay, how about this," I said. "Can I come and look at the cottage and bring my dogs with me? And if you tell me you don't want them, I'll get lost."

Reluctantly, Lucy agreed.

Just as I had hoped, Lucy—the softest of touches when it comes to animals—fell in love with Louie and Mickey on the spot, and I had a new place to live.

I should have been thrilled, but I wasn't. What the photos didn't convey was just how small the cottage was. It was twenty feet by fifteen feet, about the size of a walk-in closet in many Bedford homes. There was a kitchenette, a small bathroom, and space for a bed, a table, and a chair—and that was it. Most people would have found it cozy, charming, and perfect for a single person, but most people's lives weren't a disaster. At the time, mine was. The longest relationship of my life had just ended after eight years. I had $1,000 in the bank, a mountain of credit-card debt, and no steady job. Emotionally, I was a wreck. Finding myself in a tiny room on someone else's property seemed to affirm just how far I'd fallen. The boy who was going to be president was now the man who had nothing.

The great saving grace was Lucy. Very quickly, she became like family to me.

When Laura and I pulled onto her property and parked in the driveway between the cottage and house, Lucy came out to greet us. She was her usual bright, cheerful self, and seeing her smiling made me feel ill. How could I tell her that little Oliver, whom she had come to adore, was gone? I didn't know how to do it, didn't know how to phrase it or what tone to use, so when I got out of Laura's car I just blurted it out.

"Oliver's gone. Someone stole him."

"Oh no!" Lucy said. "Oh my God."

My legs felt weak again, so I sat down in the grass outside Lucy's house. Lucy sat down with me. She asked what had happened, and I told her the story. She tried to console me, but it wasn't much use. It was as if I'd become immune to optimism and positive thinking. There was simply no combination of words or truisms or good wishes that could make me feel less despondent. *And yet*, I thought, *people keep trying. God bless them.*

Suddenly, my sister Laura, who had been on her cell phone, came rushing over.

"Steven, you're going on TV," she said.

"What?"

"I got through to News 12. They're interested. They're going to do a segment on Oliver. Lisa Reyes, the reporter, is going to meet us outside Ralph's Cigars at 3:15 p.m."

I was stunned. Not by the fact that Laura had kept calling the station and had finally gotten through and persuaded someone to do a segment—persuading people was what she did for a living—but by how this announcement made me feel. It made me feel . . . what? Good? Hopeful? Certainly, knowing someone believed that Oliver's loss was a story worthy of TV, knowing someone *cared* that he was gone, made me feel a little bit less alone in the world. But just as quickly as that feeling came over me, it vanished. I couldn't hold on to any positivity for longer than a moment.

"Steven, you have to go shave," Laura said.

She was right. I hadn't shaved in two days, and I looked haggard. If I was going to be on TV, I had to shore myself up. I had to look presentable.

But even though I knew she was right, the bitterness I felt made me resent her. I didn't like her bossing me around and telling me what I *had* to do. Didn't Laura have even a little sympathy for me, considering what had happened? Nor did I like that everyone was being calm and acting as if the worst possible thing hadn't happened. I didn't like anything about my situation or my life, for that matter. I was angry. *Very* angry. The whole world could go to hell as far as I was concerned. So instead of thanking Laura for her concern and perseverance, I lashed out.

"Don't tell me what to do," I said.

"Steven, you have to shave. You have to—"

"Don't tell me what I have to do! I don't have to do anything! I lost Oliver! I don't care about anything!"

I stormed off to my cottage, a portrait of grief and gloom. Lucy took Laura by the arm and said, "Let him go."

Chapter Seven

I stewed in my cottage for a while, grateful that no one came to fetch me. I needed the time to pull myself together and get to a point where I could at least *pretend* to care. Finally, I got up and took a shower. I didn't give much thought to the fact that I would soon be on TV, and I put on my blue pullover and my vest, which always kept me nice and warm. Outside the cottage, I went over to Laura and apologized for how I'd acted.

"Well," she said, "you look much better now."

We got in Laura's car for the ride back to the cigar store in Scarsdale. Lucy came along for support.

"Are you going to be all right?" Laura asked me as she drove. "I mean, on TV?"

"Yes, I'll be fine," I said. "I'm ready to do this."

That was a lie.

We pulled into the parking lot where I last saw Oliver, and I felt a wave of nausea come over me. I had a bottle of water with me, and I drank it all, but I held on to the plastic bottle. I needed something in my hands; otherwise, they would shake.

A few minutes after we got there, a white van with a large satellite dish sticking out of the top pulled into the lot. It was marked

"News 12 Westchester." The passenger door opened, and Lisa Reyes hopped out. I recognized her from the nightly seven o'clock newscast. She was the on-scene reporter at car crashes, arrests, local happenings, what have you. Now she was here to cover the sad story of a stolen dog. *My* stolen dog.

Lisa came over to say hello. She was tall and pretty, with dark hair and a warm, welcoming smile, and she instantly put me at ease. I felt a sudden surge of gratitude for her presence. The last thing I wanted to do was go on television and talk about Oliver, but that was also the *best* thing I could do. And it was only possible because of Lisa's interest. She reached out for a handshake, but I hugged her instead.

The cameraman got in place outside Ralph's Cigars, and Lisa told me where to stand. She explained she was going to ask me questions about Oliver and about what happened to him. I took a deep breath and prayed I could keep my composure. Lisa motioned to the cameraman to start filming and then turned to me. I squeezed the empty water bottle in my hand and heard it crinkling.

Lisa asked me to tell her about Oliver.

"Oliver goes everywhere with me," I said. "We're inseparable. We're best friends. We were together last night, and we stopped here. I went into the cigar store for a minute, and I must have accidentally left the car door unlocked because when I came back out, Oliver was gone."

By the time I finished talking, my eyes were wet with tears.

Lisa talked about how the strip mall had no surveillance cameras, which meant there was basically no evidence to help us in the search, so we really needed the public's help in finding Oliver. Lisa referred to his theft as a "Valentine's Day caper." She turned back to me and asked me what I'd like to say to whoever had Oliver. She was asking me to plead for his return, and I did.

"This is breaking me up," I said. "I know Oliver is scared because he needs me—and I need him. I don't have kids. I'm not married. He's all I've got. Please. *Please*. We need each other."

The cameraman stopped filming. In my hand the water bottle was a crushed ball of plastic.

The News 12 crew took some footage of Laura and me putting up flyers and then drove off. The whole thing took less than half an hour. Laura said we should go into every store in the strip mall and put up flyers. I didn't think that would work because I didn't think the store owners would want our desperate flyers cluttering their walls. Laura would not be deterred. She marched into the China Buffet, the restaurant next to Ralph's. I followed her in and stayed behind her as she approached the hostess, explained about Oliver, and asked if she could put up a flyer.

"Oh my goodness, absolutely, of course you can," the hostess said without hesitation. "I feel so sorry for you. Please, put up a flyer anywhere you want."

It was the same way in every store we went into. The hair salon. The Pet Goods store. The deli. Ralph's Cigars. They all listened to our story, told us how sorry they were, and let us put up a flyer. I was taken aback. I hadn't expected such automatic kindness. These people didn't know me, yet they felt bad for me. They were rooting for me to find Oliver. They cared about me and my little dog. I was exhausted and emotionally drained, but even so, I felt an unmistakable uplift in my soul.

Eventually we got into Laura's car and drove back to Lucy's house. My day wasn't over yet. I still had a driving job to do—taking a local client, Carina, to Westchester County Airport. I'd driven for her a couple of times, and we always swapped stories about our pets. Not surprisingly, I wasn't looking forward to the job.

"Steven, you're not going anywhere," Laura said. "Lucy and I will drive your client."

"Don't be ridiculous," I said.

"We don't want you driving. It was a tough day. Stay here. We'll do it. It's no big deal."

I said okay and gave Laura the client's information. That was my sister, always there for me when I needed her. I wasn't planning on sleeping in my cottage that night—I didn't think I could bear it—so I waited in Lucy's house until Laura and Lucy came back to take us to Laura's place.

While I was waiting, my sister Nancy called and asked me if I wanted to put the story up on Facebook. I told her I had no interest in that. I wasn't much of a Facebook guy, and the thought of a bunch of strangers offering condolences didn't appeal to me. Nancy argued that it could be good to have a photo of Oliver up on Facebook. I told her I rarely went on Facebook anyway, so what was the point?

"What is there to lose?" Nancy said. "If you don't want to post it, I'll post it for you on my page. I'm always on Facebook."

"If you want to do it, God bless you. Be my guest," I finally said. "Knock yourself out."

I had no idea what Nancy posted, but a short while later she told me the story had already been shared five times.

"No, wait, eight shares," she said. "Ten shares!"

I didn't know what that meant. Was ten shares a good thing? Was that a lot? I didn't care. I just didn't see how a bunch of strangers on the internet could ever play a part in finding Oliver. What help could they possibly be?

While I was sitting in the living room, staring ahead and think-ing bitter thoughts, Lucy's husband, Alan, came down the stairs and sat next to me. I wasn't thrilled to see him. I wanted to be alone.

Alan is a sweet and lovely man, one of the nicest people I've ever known, but he's also a little shy and reserved. He doesn't talk much; it's almost as if he's decided to let Lucy do all the talking for both of them. We weren't exactly close, certainly not as close as Lucy and I had become. We'd never had a heart-to-heart or a real conversation about anything. But we got along just fine.

Alan leaned toward me and looked at me with the sad-eyed, sym-pathetic expression I had already grown tired of. "Lucy told me what happened," he said. "I'm so sorry."

"Thanks," I said.

Alan paused and took a deep, loud breath.

"You know, we don't really know why things happen in life," he said.

Oh, boy, I thought. *I just want to be alone.*

"Do you know what I think?" Alan went on. "I think there's a whole other world that goes on around us that we don't know about, and in some crazy way this other world is what protects us from really bad things happening."

I was confused. How could it protect us from really bad things? A really bad thing *had* happened.

"Look, I'm not saying that losing Oliver was a good thing," Alan said. "It's terrible. Oliver was taken from you. But we don't know the reason he was taken. If Oliver hadn't been stolen, how do you know that something even worse might not have happened?"

"What do you mean?"

"You went into that store. That decision caused a whole world to exist for you. But if you hadn't gone into that store, a whole different world would have been created. Now, we can't know this other world because it's invisible to us. But what might have happened to us in that world could have been much worse than what happened in the world where Oliver got stolen. Maybe Oliver getting stolen protected you from something even worse, like, I don't know, getting hit by a tractor trailer. Maybe this invisible alternate world was protecting you and Oliver."

I was dumbstruck. I'd never heard Alan talk like this. I'd barely heard him talk at all. Maybe we'd discuss the weather or the animals or what we had for breakfast. But this? Invisible worlds? Where was this coming from?

"Steven," Alan said, leaning in closer, "we have to trust in the things that happen *as happening for a reason*. Maybe your life was saved last night. We just don't know."

With that, Alan got up and went back upstairs.

Much later, when I told Lucy what Alan said to me in one of my darkest moments, in the depths of my despair, her reaction was that he couldn't possibly have said it.

"He doesn't talk like that," she said. "Alan doesn't go deep like that."

And yet he had, and even more remarkably, what he said somehow penetrated my brick wall of negativity.

Together with the unexpected kindness of the shop owners, Alan's strange little speech was the start of my journey to understanding that losing Oliver was not the end of something but actually just the beginning.

Chapter Eight

It was another long night, and with it came another endless loop of dread and worry, in between spurts of tortured sleep, to the point where I couldn't tell the terrible thoughts from the terrible dreams. They were all fueled by the same question.

Where is he?

Oliver's absence was like a crushing weight on my shoulders, impossible to ignore, debilitating, painful. What made it worse was what I knew about Oliver's personality—he was a gentle, sensitive dog. With other small dogs I'd had, I'd been able to horse around with them, roll in the grass, and tussle and frolic without worrying too much. They were sturdy. But Oliver was different. There was something a little fragile about him.

"He is a baby," one friend told me when I got him. "You have to be easy with him. He is your little angel."

They were right. Oliver *was* my little angel. He was sweet and sensitive. But now, whoever had Oliver didn't know this about him. And would his captor even care—or show any concern for Oliver's welfare? Or had he been stolen just for kicks?

In the dark of night, there were no answers, only more agonizing questions.

So while I sat up on Laura's sofa in the middle of the night, wide awake and worried to death, my mother's candle twinkling in the dark, I tried to channel the intense connection I had with Oliver. I wanted to know what he was thinking and how he was handling his nightmare.

That is, if he was even alive.

The one thing I kept telling myself, as I sat in the dark grasping for any assurance, was "Oliver is smart. That is in our favor." Oliver trained quickly, knew his toys by name, and knew how to look out for himself. He was playful and friendly, and he had a big, open heart, but he also knew when to back off and seek safety. He was not entirely guileless. I never put him on a leash on Lucy's property because he never wandered away or got lost. Oliver was, without question, a very smart dog.

Which matters, I told myself, *because he's in a situation where he needs to be smart.*

As soon as the car door had opened and a strange pair of arms reached in to take him, Oliver would have known that something was wrong. *This is not my dad*, he would have thought. *This is not good.*

But he wouldn't have fought his abductor; he was too small and sweet to do that. He wasn't aggressive and he wasn't a biter; he was a retreater. He wasn't even a growler. If someone approached him too abruptly or a kid rushed over and startled him, Oliver wouldn't growl like other dogs I'd had. He would run away. Maybe he'd growl a little bit when I teased him by keeping a toy away from him, but it wasn't much of a growl. And it certainly wasn't intimidating. It was more adorable than menacing.

So he wouldn't have growled or snipped or barked. He would have played it cool. Steve McQueen cool. Okay, maybe he would have trembled involuntarily, but he wouldn't have yelped or whimpered—he would have gone with the flow. Yes, that's what Oliver would have done as he was carried away from the car, carried away from me. He would have swallowed his fear and bewilderment, and he would have played along.

And when he got the chance, he would have crawled under a dresser.

Okay, I thought, playing the scene out in my mind. *So now Oliver is out of the SUV and into someone else's car.* I assumed another car was involved. Whoever took him must have had a car, I reasoned, unless it was just some local kids pulling a prank or maybe snatching Oliver because they wanted their own dog. But it all happened so quickly that I suspected it was a more professional operation: someone staking out the parking lot, seeing me leave Oliver behind, swiftly taking him out of my car, then casually driving away with him.

But why? Why would someone do that?

Well, to sell him, I figured. Little dogs go for lots of money in pet stores, and someone could probably have gotten a few hundred dollars for Oliver. He wasn't a pure breed, but he could almost have passed for one. Or, as I said, they might have taken him to keep him as their own. He was certainly cute and irresistible. Either motive was okay with me because they both required that Oliver be fed and cared for. Any other motives I refused to even consider. I had to believe that whoever took Oliver had an interest in keeping him safe and sound.

So Oliver is in the passenger seat of a stranger's car. I could picture him huddled in a little ball against the back of the seat, as far away from his abductor as he could get, wondering, *Who is this guy? Where am I going? Where is my dad?* Yes, he would be wondering all of these things. But he wouldn't panic. He would be quiet. I knew that he would do this. I had no doubt he would react this way.

How could I be so sure?

Because I knew that Oliver knew I would stop at nothing to get him back. All Oliver had to do was bide his time and play it cool.

I'll do what I'm told. I'll sit where they put me. I won't make noise. If they want to pet me, I'll let them pet me. And in time, Stee will come and get me. And then we'll go back to how it was.

Yes, I was sure of it. This was how Oliver would handle his abduction. And when I focused on this certainty, I felt a small but welcome measure of peace in my soul. Because, though I didn't dare vocalize it or dwell on the thought, I understood deep down that if Oliver did indeed play it cool and play it smart, as I knew he would, then even if I *didn't* get him back, he would be okay. Whoever took him would fall in love with him, just as I had, and they would have to take care of him and protect him from harm. So Oliver would be okay—heartbroken, for sure, as I would be, but physically safe and surely loved by someone else. And that, I understood on some deep level, would not be the worst thing that could happen, at least not for Oliver.

Which, in the middle of the dark and sleepless night, gave me something resembling comfort.

If I had just stopped there, if I could have cut off the endless loop of dread and forced myself to empty my brain and think of nothing at all, I wouldn't have started wondering what Oliver was thinking on our first night apart, when the lights went out and all went black, and he was in a strange place with strange people, and I was nowhere to be found. When both of us were alone in our new worlds, afraid and confused—*What*, I wondered, *would Oliver have thought?*

Of course, I knew the answer. As he curled up his little body and closed his little eyes tight against the night, Oliver would have thought, *Where is Stee? When will I get to see Stee?*

The Search: Day Two
February 16

Here's another thing you need to know about Oliver: he doesn't like loud noises. He doesn't like disruptions of any kind. Even when I make my bed, all the fluffing of sheets and tossing of pillows is too much for him, and he runs and hides under the dresser.

Nor can Oliver handle me being mad at him. The one time I scolded him after he tore down the headliner in my Oldsmobile Cutlass, he crawled under the car and stayed there for half an hour. I got on my hands and knees in the driveway and pleaded with him to come out, but he just moved farther away, nursing his hurt feelings. When I finally coaxed him out, I hugged him tight and promised I'd never get mad at him again.

I kept that promise and never raised my voice to him again. Not that I ever needed to. I mean, seriously, how could I ever get angry at that sweet little face?

Chapter Nine

I woke up in another dark mood. Never mind that the day before, Laura and I felt as if we'd scored a little victory by getting our story on News 12. When we watched Lisa Reyes's short, dramatic segment, it gave us all a shot of hope. But then the night silence taunted me every second: Why wasn't the phone ringing? Why hadn't Oliver already been found? Had anybody even seen the report? And in the harsh light of day, my little scraps of hope seemed measly and pathetic.

Nancy called and said she was driving up from Brooklyn, where she lived, to spend the day with Laura and me and help in any way she could.

"Nancy, you don't have to do that," I said.

"Steven, I am coming."

I also got a call from an old friend, Eric Weinstein. Eric and I knew each other from back in Huntington Station, where we'd attended junior high and Walt Whitman High School together. Eric grew up down the street from me, and I knew him to be a hustling hard worker, even at an early age. He was always either doing a job or looking for more jobs. Whenever I thought of him, I thought of the Beatles' song "Eight Days a Week." That was Eric, working and hustling eight days a week.

Eric had a paper route in town when we were kids, and he helped me get one too—my very first job. Early Sunday mornings we'd meet in his garage and sort through a stack of thick *Newsdays*. We'd stuff our canvas bags full of them, sling the bags over the handlebars of our bikes, and ride off on our routes. Eric had one of those bikes with huge handlebars, so the heavy Sunday papers didn't seem to be much of a problem for him. My bike had regular handlebars, and the Sunday papers weighed me down so much, I felt like I was pedaling through mud.

After high school Eric and I went to different colleges, and our friendship sputtered to a stop. For some reason, we didn't talk for the next thirty years. We just went our own ways, I guess. But then, in 2013, out of the blue, Eric called me. I was in pretty bad shape at the time—mentally, emotionally, financially, every which way—so I was happy to hear from my old pal. Eric told me that he, too, was miserable. He'd just been fired from his job as a risk-assessment officer at a bank in New York, and he was feeling pretty low. We commiserated for a while, relieved just a bit by our shared bad fortune.

"Listen," Eric said, "I'm doing a gig at a catering hall next month. Why don't you come out and work as a bartender?"

Eric, the consummate hustler, worked as both a restaurant maître d' and a caterer at night, even while he worked full-time at the bank, so he still had those jobs to fall back on. His offer thrilled me because I'd always secretly wanted to be a bartender. I'd watched my father operate behind a bar and had seen how much everyone liked and admired him. I used to think he had the coolest job in the world. But my father never had the patience to teach me to mix drinks, nor did he suggest bartending as a job I might be able to handle. Helping me acquire life skills just wasn't something he did.

"Eric, I've never mixed a drink in my life. I don't think I can do it," I said.

"What are you talking about? Scotch and soda. Jack and soda. Beer. You'll learn."

The catering hall was way out in Mineola on Long Island, a long drive from Bedford, but something told me the bartending job would be good for me, so I said yes. Being around people, feeling confident behind the bar, the chance to identify with my father—those seemed like necessary things for me at a time when my self-esteem was at its lowest. I began to look forward to working alongside Eric. It would be like old times, the two of us laughing it up in his garage. A few days later, I met Eric in Mineola, and we went to see the manager of the catering hall about bartending a big wedding.

"I can only use one of you," the manager declared.

I was deflated and got up to leave.

"Take him," Eric said, pointing to me.

I told Eric that was silly, that this was his job and he should take it.

"You need it more than I do," he said. "Just take it."

Reluctantly, I agreed. I went home and watched YouTube videos about making drinks, and on the day of the wedding I bartended by myself. I was thrown right into cocktail hour without a word of instruction, and I was terrified—I didn't even know how to slice a lemon. But I hung in there and kept mixing drinks. The patrons could see I didn't know what I was doing, but they were nice and encouraging about it. And by the end of the night, I was cranking out shots and highballs at a more-than-respectable pace. I made it through my first gig, and as I'd suspected, it *was* good for me. It *did* boost my confidence. Plus, I made more than a hundred dollars in tips, which really helped financially. And it wouldn't have happened if it hadn't been for my friend Eric.

Now, six years later, Eric was calling because I'd left him a message that Oliver was gone, and he was insisting that he would come up from Amityville, Long Island—a brutal sixty-mile drive—to be with me and help me look for Oliver.

"Eric, don't be crazy. You don't have to come," I said.

"Steven, you're my friend," he said. "I'm coming."

Our little search party was starting to grow.

Before I could spend time with Nancy and Eric, though, I had another driving job to do. It had been on the books for a while, and it was for clients who were also friends—Beth and Wyatt and their two young children, Belle and Wilson—so I couldn't cancel it. Ironically, we had bonded as friends through our pets when I did some pet sitting for their dachshund, Gus, in my cottage. The only problem I had with Gus was his fondness for rooting through bags of groceries. My guys knew to stay away from shopping bags I brought into the cottage, but Gus didn't. So if I made a second trip to the car, I'd come back and find a bag ripped open and Gus enjoying an early lunch of raw steak.

That day, I had to take the family from Bedford to the airport in Newark, New Jersey, a trip that would take ninety minutes each way. Before I left Laura's house to pick them up, Laura asked me not to talk about Oliver during the drive.

"You can see how devastating this is for all of us," she said. "Beth and Wyatt know Oliver, and so do the kids. Maybe don't bring it up so they don't get all sad before their vacation."

I knew she was right. Nancy had almost thrown up when she heard Oliver was gone. Nancy's daughter, Jena, who adored Oliver, was also badly broken up. Another client of mine was so upset she kept checking in with me every few hours to see how I was doing. It wouldn't be fair to Beth and Wyatt's kids, who loved playing with Oliver whenever they saw him, to tell them Oliver had been stolen and was missing. I promised Laura I'd keep my mouth shut. But I also didn't know what I'd do if—or, more likely, when—they asked me about Oliver.

In the SUV I put on my sunglasses to hide my eyes. I'd been crying on and off for two days, and it showed. With a forced smile on my face, I picked up Beth and Wyatt and their kids, and we set off for the airport. We chatted about their vacation and how much fun it would be. I talked golf with Wyatt and traded trivia questions with Wilson. And then the dreaded moment came when we pulled into a gas station to get some treats for the road.

"So how is Oliver?" Beth asked, a big smile on her face.

I turned around slowly with my sunglasses still on.

"Oh, he's good," I said. "You know Oliver. Probably sleeping soundly right now."

"That's good," Beth said. "Say hello to him for us when you get home, okay?"

"I sure will," I said, hoping she couldn't see the tears forming in my eyes through my sunglasses.

No one mentioned Oliver for the rest of the trip. I kept up as brave a front as I could. But during the drive, I started seething inside. Having to pretend that everything was okay was eating away at me. So I resumed my sporadic inner dialogue with God.

Okay, so I have to be the brave one, is that it? I have to be strong and stalwart and pretend Oliver is just fine so nobody else gets upset. Is that it, God? Fine. You want me to play this game, I'll play this game. But don't kid me that you love me. Don't tell me that you care about me. Because you took my dog.

You. Took. My. Dog.

The last few days of my mother's illness were the worst. Earlier on, she had found ways to stay busy while confined to her recliner in the den. She knitted me a beautiful brown afghan blanket that I still have forty years later. She ran out of thread two-thirds of the way through and knitted the last third in a slightly darker shade of brown. Every time I see the subtle change in color on the blanket, I smile and think of my mother. For a while she made creative papier-mâché angels using an empty dishwashing-liquid bottle as a base. She also fashioned Christmas wreaths with pinecones I gathered from a neighbor's yard. She'd fasten the cones to a metal ring and put bells and red ribbons and gold ornaments on them as finishing touches. They were beautiful.

But then all the arts and crafts stopped.

Toward the end, my mother's life became all about survival—or, really, waiting to die. One night in October 1976, out of the blue, she asked me to play the organ for her, as I had done so many times before. I played exactly three songs, all her favorites—"Spanish Eyes" by Engelbert Humperdinck, Bobby Vinton's "My Melody of Love," and her absolute favorite "And I Love You So," a Perry Como standard. I remember playing the last song as slowly as I could because I didn't want the moment to end. I didn't want to ever stop playing songs for her.

The next morning paramedics came to our house and rushed my mother to the Memorial Sloan Kettering hospital in New York City. I was able to see her one final time that day. I stood by her bed in her hospital room, with my father on the other side of the bed, as she spoke with us.

"Take care of Steven," she told my father. "He is a special boy. Be good to him."

My dad looked at me and nodded. It was his way of telling me he would do his best to honor my mother's wish. And though I knew there would be hard times ahead, I believed he meant it. My father was a good man. The disease he had was another matter.

Then my mother told me she would always be there with me and for me, just in a different way than I was used to.

I believed her too.

My mother died three days later, on October 13, 1976.

I was thirteen years old. My mother was forty-seven.

Up until the moment she passed, I later realized, I'd thought of myself as special. I was loved and championed by my parents, especially my mother, and I felt like I had been chosen for something great in life. Grown-ups thought I was smart and funny and charming, and I felt comfortable in my skin. I had confidence to spare. I could hardly wait for my future to unfold.

But when my mother died, that all changed. The feeling of being special went away. The confidence and optimism disappeared, replaced by feelings of loss, abandonment, and inferiority. I was no longer comfortable in my own skin.

I wouldn't feel comfortable again for forty years.

We made it to Newark Liberty International Airport on schedule, and I got out of the SUV and said goodbye to Beth and Wyatt and the kids. I wished them a happy vacation and waved as they disappeared into the terminal. Then I slumped back into the SUV and glumly drove the sixty-two miles home, resuming my bitter conversation with God.

"Are you satisfied?" I asked him aloud, punctuating my words with fist shakes and angry gestures. "I did a nice thing, and I didn't ruin their vacation. Is that what you wanted? Fine, I did it. But understand this: I'm done with you now. I'm done with all of you. As far as I'm concerned, all of you up there—Mom, Dad, my brother, you, God—I'm finished with you all."

Anyone who happened to look over at me on the New Jersey Turnpike at that moment would have seen a troubled man, his face contorted, his fists banging on the steering wheel, and they would have thought, as they carefully steered away from me, *Wow, that guy is nuts.*

I guess you could call it road rage, though I wasn't mad at anyone on the road. I was mad at everyone *in the universe.*

Chapter Ten

When I got back to Laura's house, Nancy was there. She'd made the long drive up to be with us. When I was a kid, Nancy and I were not close. She was only five years older than me, but that was enough of a gap to keep us from being buddies. Basically, I was a pest who couldn't help annoying her and her girlfriends. Whenever they'd come over to our house and hang out in Nancy's bedroom, I'd attach my suction-cup tape recorder to the telephone in the living room and try to tape their calls. I had to pick up the receiver very delicately so they wouldn't hear me tinkering with it, but inevitably they did, and I'd hear Nancy scream, "Steven, stop trying to tape us!"

When we got older, though, Nancy and I bonded over the shared challenge of dealing with our unpredictable dad. Nancy knew that while my father was giving me driving lessons, he was being hard on me, so she took over and taught me how to drive a stick shift in her really cool orange 1973 Volkswagen Beetle. Sometimes she'd let me borrow the Bug so I could drive my friends around in it. Nancy and I even went to the same college for one year. We both chose the college for the same reason—it was just about the farthest away we could get from our home and still be in the state of New York.

When Nancy saw me walk into Laura's house, she came over and gave me a big, long hug. I melted into it. She told me she was praying for me, and so were her husband, John, her daughter, Jena, and her son, Christian. I thanked her and told her it felt really good to have her there.

Not much later, my friend Eric also showed up at Laura's. Years ago we'd both been awkward, goofy kids who wore thick glasses and had no chance with the pretty girls. But after college, Eric lifted weights and became incredibly fit, and at fifty-five he still was. Smart and quick-witted, Eric could tell you a joke on any topic—eating, sleeping, dancing. I swear, he could have been a professional stand-up comic, but he was always too busy with his many jobs to give it a shot. When I saw him walk through Laura's front door, I felt the tension drain from my body. He was *exactly* the person I needed to have around at that moment.

I apologized to Eric for dragging him away from work just to be with me.

"Don't worry about it," Eric said. "I had a little run-in with my catering boss a couple of weeks ago, and I quit."

Quitting his job was what made it possible for Eric to be there with me. The guy who never stopped working, had stopped working—at least long enough to have some free time *just* when Oliver went missing. *Wow*, I thought, *what a weird coincidence*.

Laura printed out fifty more flyers, and she and Nancy drove to Scarsdale to put them up in the area where Oliver had been stolen—on shop windows, telephone poles, bulletin boards, everywhere they could. Eric and I were tasked with calling all the veterinarians and animal hospitals in the area to ask about Oliver, let them know he had been stolen, and give them a description in case anyone brought him in. We drove around in Eric's car while I made the calls.

"Hey, does Oliver have a chip?" Eric asked. "You know, one of those implanted chip things?"

"I don't know. I can't find his paperwork."

"So call the place where you got him. They'll know."

I called the pet store in Huntington where I bought Oliver, and sure enough, they told me he did have an implanted identification chip. Okay, so now we knew that. But how was it going to help me find Oliver? Those chips weren't homing devices. They couldn't pinpoint his location. I wasn't sure what good Oliver's chip would do.

"Call the chip company," the man at the pet store told me. "They'll put an alert on him. If he is brought into any vet or shelter, they will run a scan on the dog, and an alarm will sound to let them know the dog is lost or stolen."

So that's what I did. I had the chip manufacturer put an alert on Oliver. It felt like a real accomplishment. We were covering the bases. Working all angles. It felt good.

But only for a moment, before the gloom returned.

I wasn't allowed to cry at the funeral. My father didn't permit it. He told me he needed me to be strong for the family. So I steeled myself for a grueling three-day ordeal: two long days of viewing at the funeral home, followed by a mass and burial on the third day. I was happy that so much was being done to honor my mother, but for me, a thirteen-year-old kid, the whole process was incredibly daunting—especially since my mother's casket would be half-open. The thought of seeing her in her coffin terrified me.

The day before the first viewing, Nancy took me to a store in

Huntington to buy me dress shoes for the funeral. The salesman measured my foot in that metal contraption and went downstairs to fetch the shoes. I sat and waited, absently listening to the elevator music piping into the store. One song ended and another began, and suddenly the music sounded familiar. It was a tune I recognized. I tried to place it, and finally I did: it was an instrumental version of "And I Love You So."

The last song I played for my mother just days earlier.

The realization hit me hard. My whole body began to tremble involuntarily, and my eyes filled with tears. Nancy rushed over and asked me what was wrong.

"The song!" I yelled out. "The song, the song! It's her! It's Mom! Why is this song playing now?"

I was so emotionally overcome, Nancy had to take me out of the store to calm me down. A few minutes later we went back in and paid for my new shoes. I left feeling that my mother's favorite song playing in the store at precisely the moment I was there was not a mere coincidence. No, I saw it as a sign. A sign from my mother. An affirmation that she was, just as she'd promised, by my side, forever and always. Regardless of what the world chose to throw at me, my mother would be there to give me the strength to get through it. Even if it was three long days of mourning her loss.

I think it was thanks to my mother that I made it through the whole funeral process without crying in front of my family. Even when I went up to her coffin to say goodbye, I didn't cry. My father led me up and told me to say a prayer. I knelt in front of the casket and, for the first time, looked at her.

My mother was wearing the same pink dress she wore to my sister Annette's wedding four years earlier. But while I recognized the dress, I did not recognize her. She didn't look like the person I knew.

And then, as I stared at her, I could have sworn I saw her breathing. I was sure her chest was going up and down. When I looked harder, I could tell she wasn't breathing at all. She was perfectly still, with her hands clasped around her rosary.

Slowly, I reached out and touched her hand, and I was shocked that it was ice cold. I pulled away, but then I touched her hand again. I needed to know that this was her body, but that she was already gone. Or perhaps I felt that the heat from my hands would transfer over to her and warm her up. After a minute, my father came up and gently ushered me away from the casket. I went to my seat in the first pew and sat there for the next three hours, watching my mother's friends and relatives weep and cry as they knelt at her casket and said their goodbyes. But I didn't shed a tear. Not a single one.

During the second night of viewing, my father let my mother's good friend Lillian take me to Carvel for an ice cream cone. It felt really good to get out of the funeral home. But as soon as I got in Lillian's car and closed the door behind me, I started to cry. I couldn't help it. I cried and cried and didn't stop. I wasn't allowed to cry in front of my family, but Lillian was only a good friend, so in the privacy of her car, I let it all out—all the pain and anguish and emotion, all the horrible, unanswerable questions. *Why did Mom have to leave me? Why did she have to die at such a young age? What am I going to do without her?* I cried until I couldn't cry anymore.

Thankfully, Lillian was extremely supportive. She sat there and let me get it all out of my system, and she assured me everything would be okay. I'm not sure she realized what a wonderful thing she was doing for me by taking me away from my father for a few minutes so I could finally cry. Or maybe it was my mother, all the way from heaven, who somehow gave Lillian the idea to do it, just as she had let me know that she was right there with me at the shoe store.

After driving around and making calls for two hours, Eric pulled us into a Dunkin' Donuts. We ordered our coffees and sat at a table by the window. I was silent and stared into the dark-brown pool in my cup. Eric looked at me with concern.

"Steven, I have to say, I'm worried about you," he said. "I watched you when you were looking out the car window, and it scared me. You were gone. You weren't even there. You're not here now. I've never seen you this bad, Steven, not even when your mom died."

I didn't say anything. What was there to say? I was in a bad way, and I knew it. Eric had seen me at other low points in my life, but this was different. Losing Oliver set off a chain reaction of regret and anger and self-pity that upended the very foundation of my life. It summoned a lifetime of mistakes and grudges and failings and buried me inside them. The unfairness of it all was staggering. I felt like I was all alone in my exorbitant grief and sorrow.

"I'll be okay" was the best response I could muster.

We drove back to Laura's house without saying much. Laura and Nancy were back from putting up flyers. Nancy came over with a smile on her face.

"The Oliver post is up to three hundred shares!" she said.

"Is that good?" I asked.

"It's unheard of," Nancy said. "That's a lot of people who had shared a little local story. And look what they're saying."

Nancy showed me some of the comments below the post. I'd

been adamant that I didn't want sympathy from strangers, but these comments went beyond sympathy:

> I don't even know you personally, but I am home right now with my dog, and I am crying my eyes out for you.

> This breaks my heart. Please tell Steven I am saying my prayers that he finds Oliver soon.

> I can't stop crying. Steven, please let me know if there's anything I can do to help you get Oliver back.

There were dozens and dozens of comments just like these. Reading them knocked the wind out of me, and I had to sit down. These weren't just random well-wishers tossing off kind comments. These were people speaking from the heart and sharing their own distress over what had happened. These were people who were *crying*, just like I was. They didn't know Oliver or me, yet they experienced real pain and sadness over our separation.

To be honest, I was astonished that anyone would take such an interest in our story, much less express such empathy for what we were going through. Suddenly, losing Oliver didn't feel like it was my own private, impenetrable agony. Our story had touched the hearts of all these people, almost as if it had happened to them. How was this possible? Why did people care so much about some guy and his dog? What was happening?

And then I thought, *Maybe I'm not as alone in this thing as I think I am.*

I changed my mind about the Facebook post and gave Nancy some new pictures of Oliver to put up. I didn't want to post anything myself, but I was okay with Nancy keeping the story current and sharing any news with followers. I could see that all of us—Nancy, Laura, Eric, and I—felt energized by the reaction on Facebook. But I could also tell that though I was inspired by the support, I was less energized than the others. Losing Oliver was always going to be more personal to me because, after all, he was my dog. So I didn't get quite as excited by incremental progress as the rest of our little team. That was just the way it was going to be.

It was getting late, and I walked Eric to his car. Before he got in, he turned to me and gave me an enormous hug. Then he stepped back and looked at me.

"Steven, don't you see who you are?" he asked. "You're George Bailey!"

"What are you talking about?"

"George Bailey. From *It's a Wonderful Life*. He had to lose everything before he could see how truly loved he was. He almost jumped off a bridge because things were so bad. Maybe that's you, Steven. Maybe you're George Bailey, and you don't even know it!"

I was surprised to hear Eric talking this way. Like Lucy's husband, Alan, Eric wasn't exactly Mr. Philosophy. But what he was saying did make some kind of sense to me. I mean, I couldn't deny that people were rallying to my side. My sisters. My friends. The strip mall shop owners. Three hundred strangers on Facebook. People were stepping forward and giving me advice and support and encouragement and, yes, love.

"Steven, you're a good guy, and people love you," Eric went on. "Maybe you really needed to see just how much people love you. Maybe that's why Oliver was taken, so you could see it. Steven, I believe you're going to get Oliver back. But this whole thing—this is about your *journey*, man."

I hugged Eric, then watched him drive away. When I went back inside Laura's house, Nancy rushed over again.

"We're up to five hundred shares, Steven!"

By the next morning, the number of people who had shared our story was more than a thousand.

The Search: Day Three
February 17

Oliver knows all my moves. He knows what each twitch, each gesture means. If I'm getting ready to go out and fixing my tie in a mirror, Oliver will sit on the bed, rapt and motionless, watching me and waiting for his cue. Is Stee taking me with him? Or am I staying behind? Come on, come on, give me the sign. And all I have to do is look at him in a particular way, with a particular slight arch of an eyebrow, and Oliver will know. He will jump off the bed and spin like a top and grab his little stuffed blue hippo or brown bear and take it with him to the door. He'll know that he's coming with me, and all will be well with his world.

This is how we do much of our communicating. I reach for something; he knows what it means. I move a certain way; he knows what's going to happen. Imagine being that connected to someone. Imagine if we were all connected that way.

Chapter Eleven

On Sunday morning, Nancy drove back up from Brooklyn to hang more flyers in Scarsdale. I told her again that she didn't have to come all the way up, but she insisted. Meanwhile, Laura drove into Manhattan for her part-time job as a sales associate at Tiffany, the famed Fifth Avenue flagship store. For her, it was the perfect post-career job—one where she got to put her great taste, love of fine things, and ability to sell anything to great use. I was glad she'd be doing something that would take her mind off Oliver. She'd been going nonstop for two days, and I felt a change of pace would be good.

I needed a break too. The intensity of the past two days—and the complete absence of any information about Oliver and where he might be—was tearing me apart. I walked around feeling as if I might burst into tears at any moment. Awake, I was restless and miserable; asleep, I was plagued by nightmares. I needed to break the pattern, if only for a short while. As hard as it was to do, I decided to take a quick respite from searching for Oliver and go to my local gym.

I drove from Laura's house to my cottage and packed some work-out clothes in my gym bag. I brought along my earphones and my workout music. I'd been pretty good about staying in shape the past few years, and I'd come to really enjoy hopping on the treadmill and sweating to the beat of my favorite songs—classics by Dion, the Shirelles, Fats Domino, Earl (Speedo) Carroll, and the Cadillacs to name a few. It was cleansing and reinvigorating, and, Lord knows, I needed a little bit of reinvigoration right about then.

But the instant I walked into my gym, I knew I wouldn't be able to work out at all. I used to do a vigorous routine on the treadmill and the VersaClimber, propelled by the music I loved so dearly piping through my earphones. My routine was joyful. But before I even got out on the gym floor, I knew I would not be able to summon my usual enthusiasm for the workout. How could I throw myself into it while knowing that Oliver wasn't at home, that Oliver was out there somewhere, waiting for me to find him? In an instant, I realized I hadn't only lost my dog; I'd lost my workouts, my music, my routine.

I'd lost everything.

I found the energy to take a steam bath and shower, but that was it. Sullenly, I drove back home. I got out of the car and forced myself to take a walk along East Field Drive, which ran along Lucy's property. But after about fifty steps, I found I couldn't do that either. East Field Drive was where Oliver and I would take our long morning hikes. Without him there, I didn't have the slightest desire to go another step. On an ordinary day, Oliver and I would have followed our hike with a visit to my dear neighbors, Sherman and Bzee Durfee, who sometimes babysat Oliver for me when my schedule got hectic. But on that day, the Durfees were in Florida, and I was spared the awful task of telling them Oliver was stolen. With no Oliver and no Durfees and nowhere else to go, I fell to my knees on the dirt path and once again wondered why this had happened to me. What was I going to learn from this seemingly random and pointless loss? I got up, turned around, and slunk back home.

What cruel transformation was overtaking me? It wasn't too hard to figure out. Losing Oliver had destroyed my spirit. It had sapped me of purpose and desire. It was like stripping the engine out of a car—all that's left is a useless shell.

"So I guess this is it," I said aloud on my way to the cottage. "This is my life now. Go to work, come home, try to sleep. If I don't get Oliver back, this will be my life."

And then another thought: *You know what, Dad? I guess you were right. I guess this is the Carino way.*

When I was little I was never afraid that my father would physically hurt me. In his rages, he could be rough with my mother and my older brother, Frankie, but he never laid a hand on me—with one exception. It was the afternoon when I was playing with a friend on the bed of my father's Willys Jeep pickup truck and decided to funnel a handful of sand into the gas tank. I was four or five years old, and I guess I thought it would be funny. When my father figured out I'd wrecked his engine, he grabbed me by the wrist, nearly lifted me in the air, and gave me a hard boot in the butt. I don't think it hurt much, but I can still remember how humiliating it was. It's one of those moments that replays in my mind at random times, the image as sharp as ever, summoning the same humiliation I felt when I was a kid.

Other than that one time, however, my father never raised a hand to me. But he had other ways he could hurt us, and after my mother passed, I was much more in his sights than I'd ever been. Before, my mother and sisters had always shielded me from Dad at his worst. But now that my mother was gone, and my two older sisters had gotten married and moved out of the house, I had to find my own way to handle my father's wrath.

What I came to understand was that my father was full of resentments, born of events I couldn't have known about back then. He lost his own father when he was young, and during World War II he flew fifty-five successful combat missions, often being forced to drop bombs on his parents' home country, Italy. He was a decorated war veteran, but—aside from a story about how a piece of shrapnel from a bomb left a scar on his neck—he never, ever spoke about his wartime experiences or how they affected him. Only later would I understand how they might have left a part of him broken and led him to tear down his children instead of building us up and filling us with confidence. My father didn't like anyone thriving under his wing.

When I was sixteen, he began teaching me how to drive. If I made any little mistake, he'd chew me out so bad that it would make me sick. *You're driving too fast. You're driving too slow. You didn't make that turn right. What's the matter with you?*

It didn't help that I knew my father to be an excellent, confident driver. I'd watch with awe as he rolled his big Lincoln or Cadillac through a tollbooth and, without stopping, take some change in his left hand and smoothly toss it in the toll basket, all in one elegant gesture. Every time, I thought, *Wow, that is cool. I'm going to do that too.*

I got the chance when my father and I took a trip to Florida in 1981, and he let me drive on Florida's Turnpike. I had two quarters ready in my hand, but at the tollbooth I got nervous and stopped the car to throw the change instead of tossing it while driving slowly. I probably stopped for all of three seconds.

"What the hell are you stopping the car for!" my father screamed at me from the passenger seat, throwing in a few f-bombs to further his point. "What is wrong with you?"

"I didn't want to miss!" I pleaded.

"You don't stop the car; you just throw the change."

"I only stopped for three seconds."

"You shouldn't have to stop at all."

"Relax, I got the change in, didn't I?"

"I knew you couldn't do it," my father concluded with a dismissive wave of his hand.

I got another chance the following day. I slipped behind the wheel of my father's enormous 1974 Lincoln Continental Mark IV, which had a hood the size of a dining room table. When we approached the tollbooth, I collected two quarters from my pocket and carefully transferred them to my left hand. Then I rolled down the window and slowed down as I maneuvered up to the basket, careful not to stop.

With a precise swoop of my left hand, I tossed the quarters at the basket—and missed.

And because I didn't stop in time, the motorized gate arm crashed down on our oversize hood.

And then—

"What in holy hell is wrong with you!"

I scampered out of the car to pick up the quarters.

"What the hell are you doing?"

"I'm picking up the quarters!"

"Don't pick up the quarters. You're holding up the line!"

"I got it, Dad."

"Here's two quarters. Put these in!"

"Dad, I got it."

"Get back in the car and put these in! What's the matter with you? You can't even hit the basket from two feet away?"

"You made me a nervous wreck, Dad. How am I supposed to concentrate?"

I swear, our driving lessons were like a twisted comedy routine straight out of *The Honeymooners*, with me as Ed Norton and Dad as Ralph Kramden.

These moments of degradation weren't limited to our failures, though. They came even when we accomplished things we were proud of.

When Frankie came home with a new Volkswagen Beetle he worked very hard to buy, my father lit into him.

"You just threw away all your money," he said. "That's the worst car you could have ever bought."

Watching Frankie's face drop and his shoulders slump was painful. I felt so bad for him. There was no use arguing with my father; that would only make it worse. All you could do was accept the humiliation and walk away defeated.

When I got to Walt Whitman High School, I found a job working at the Mobil gas station on Jericho Turnpike. It felt like a real adult job, and I was proud and delighted to have it, despite how dirty I'd be at the end of my shift. Then I told my father about it.

"That is the worst place any person can ever work," he said. "That's a terrible job. Why would you ever work there?"

In time I learned not to share any of my accomplishments with my father. If I got the high score in pinball with my friends, I kept it to myself. If I aced a math quiz, I stuffed the test in my book bag and forgot about it. This way, my father wouldn't be able to knock me down with insults. All I had to do was conceal the best and happiest moments of my life, and I'd be fine. I realized it was safer to be a total nobody in my father's eyes.

The consequence of that strategy, though, was that eventually

I lost interest in having any achievements at all. In Little League I begged the coach not to put me in the games, and I finally quit altogether. I also gave up on my organ lessons. In high school I was a really good bowler, but when I tried out for the team, I purposefully choked in the final two frames so I wouldn't make the squad—partly because I didn't want to have to ask my father to drive me to the matches. I felt like no matter what I did, it wouldn't be good enough for my father, so why even bother? I was doing what I needed to do to survive in my dysfunctional family—and what I needed to do was nothing. I began to go through life with no passion or fervor, since there seemed to be no reward for investing myself in anything.

A pattern developed. In the broad scheme of my life, I would take one step forward and two steps back. This was the message my father instilled in us—that a Carino would never amount to anything. That a Carino might get close to succeeding but then find some way to screw it up because that's just what a Carino did. One step forward, two steps back—that was the Carino way.

That was why, when I lost Oliver, part of me wasn't even surprised. *Okay, now they're playing my song,* I thought. *This is the theme of my life. Of course, Oliver is gone. Why wouldn't he be? Get something good and screw it up. That's the Carino way.*

On Sunday evening I had an airport run, and I returned to Laura's house around nine thirty. Laura was there, back from her day at work. We sat down to dinner and talked about what we could do next to find Oliver. My heart wasn't in it, but I went along with the discussion. Oliver had been gone for three days now, and we hadn't found a single clue as to his whereabouts. Laura didn't appear to have lost any hope at all, and I was careful not to betray how hopeless I felt.

A little while later, Laura got a call on her cell. I could tell she knew the caller and was surprised to hear from whoever was on the other end. After a minute or two, she came over and gave me the phone.

"Steven, it's Uncle Pat," she said.

"Uncle Pat? What's he calling for?"

"He heard about Oliver."

Uncle Pat is my mother's brother, and he lives in Delaware with his wife, Rita. Laura and I had visited him there about a year earlier, but after that we hadn't talked at all. We weren't estranged or anything; we'd just fallen out of touch. So I was as surprised as Laura to hear from him now.

"Steven, I'm so sorry about Oliver," Uncle Pat said. "I saw it on Nancy's Facebook page, and it broke my heart. I'm sitting here now with my two little babies on my belly, and I know how much Oliver means to you. And I am just so sorry."

Uncle Pat's two babies were a pair of adorable miniature pinschers both he and Rita loved dearly and doted on.

"Steven, you have to get Oliver back," he went on.

"We're working on it, Uncle Pat," I said.

"What's the reward number?"

I told him we were offering $2,500.

"Make it $5,000," Pat said. "I'll send you a check."

"Uncle Pat, you don't have to do that."

"Steven, let me do it. Double the reward. Then do whatever you have to do to get back that dog. You've had more than your share of troubles in your life, and I'd feel guilty if I didn't do something to help you out."

The next morning Nancy updated her Facebook post and changed the reward to $5,000.

"NO QUESTIONS ASKED," she wrote. "We are up to 3,700 shares . . . amazing! Please, keep sharing. Maybe your share will be the one that brings Oliver home."

The Search: Day Four
February 18

I mentioned that Oliver doesn't like loud sounds. There is one exception, though, and that's music.

Oliver is okay when I play my music a little loud. When he sees me go to my red Planar 3 turntable in the cottage, he jumps straight up onto the bed and settles in. "Want to listen to some Elvis this morning?" I'll ask. "Or maybe Sam Cooke?" Oliver indicates he's okay with either one. I put on the record, lower the needle, and turn the volume up to around six or seven, which in a small room is pretty loud. But I prefer it that way, and, like I said, Oliver doesn't seem to mind. His ears go up, and he pays attention to the music. He doesn't mind if I start to sing along either. I have the very distinct feeling that Oliver likes the same kind of music I do.

When a certain song triggers a certain emotion, as songs sometimes do, and I start to get a little teary eyed, Oliver looks at me to make sure I'm okay, then goes back to listening. He knows the difference between me being sad and me being moved by the power of the music. Sometimes a song will remind me how lucky I am to be alive and have Oliver, and I'll get a little misty, and he understands that too. Oliver is fine with happy tears.

Chapter Twelve

The day after Oliver disappeared, someone who was trying to be helpful told me they hoped I'd find Oliver in the next three days.

"After that," the person said, "the odds get really terrible."

I thought about that when I woke up on my fourth day without Oliver—Presidents' Day, of all days. Not only did I not have Oliver, but I didn't have the slightest idea where he was or what might have happened to him. I'd received a few texts from friends and colleagues who'd seen the News 12 TV report, but none from anyone who had information about Oliver. The case of the stolen dog was stone cold.

Even so, on Monday morning I didn't feel quite as defeated as I'd figured I would. Hearing from Uncle Pat and receiving his $2,500 contribution softened some of my anger. Here was someone I hadn't bothered to call for a year, reaching out precisely when I needed him most. He and Rita were acting out of love—love for their own precious puppies, love for me, love for Oliver. How could I not be affected by such a display of love? Their gesture was another little event— along with the store owners' empathy, Alan's thoughtful words, and Eric's George Bailey speech—that opened my eyes to a simple truth: I wasn't as alone in my search for Oliver as I thought I was.

I drove to the local Kinko's in White Plains and ran off one hundred copies of the flyer, updated with the new reward.

"Sorry to hear about your dog," the guy behind the counter said.

"Oh, thanks."

"I hope you get him back. I'm pulling for you."

I smiled and put him on the list of positive encounters.

Back at Laura's house, my sister and I sat down and planned the day. I had three separate driving jobs, so I'd be out of commission all day. Laura would take the flyers to Scarsdale and hand one to everybody who came into the China Buffet.

"Steven, do you have any cute pictures or videos of Oliver we could send to Lisa Reyes at News 12?" Laura asked.

"Lemme look," I said.

On my phone I found a video of Oliver getting chased around Lucy's driveway by her cat. It was cute and funny, and I couldn't bear to watch it all the way through.

"How's this?" I asked.

"Perfect," Laura said. "This shows how precious Oliver's life was on the farm with you. I'll send it to Lisa. Maybe she'll run an update on Oliver."

A call came in on my cell, and I looked at the number. It wasn't familiar. I felt my heart seize up. Could this possibly be an Oliver sighting?

"Hi. Who is this?" I asked.

The answer came in a child's voice. A child who was crying.

"I'm Helen," she said. "Are you Steven?"

"Yes, I'm Steven."

"I got your number from a poster. I just wanted to tell you that I am so sad you can't find Oliver. I love my own dog so much, and I can't imagine someone taking him. I want to send you a picture of my dog so you'll feel better."

She sounded as if she was maybe ten years old. She was crying and sniffling through the whole call. I was disappointed it wasn't a tip, but I was also overwhelmed by Helen's kind and innocent heart.

"Thank you, Helen," I said. "And I'll send you a picture of Oliver too."

"Okay, that would be great. I really want you to find him. I'm, like, praying you find him really soon."

"Me too," I said. "Me too."

A few seconds later, I got Helen's text. She sent me a photo of her with a beautiful white Labrador. She looked so happy in the photo, and so did the Lab. I put my phone away.

I picked up my first client in Katonah and drove her to LaGuardia Airport. After dropping her off, I drove to JFK, fifteen miles away, where I would pick up my second client. I got there two hours early, which, for better or worse, gave me plenty of time to sit in the parking lot and think.

After about an hour, I had the sudden thought that I'd forgotten to call my landlady, Lucy, to ask her to let Oliver out for a walk, like I usually did when I was away all day.

Then, just as quickly, I realized I didn't have to.

I don't know why, but the second realization shocked me all over again. It hit me so hard, I had to get out of the car and walk around the parking lot. *Steven, you don't have to call Lucy about Oliver because Oliver isn't there,* I reminded myself as I paced, deafening planes flying low just over my head. *You never have to worry about Oliver again. You're a free agent now. You're free to do whatever you please. You can take any driving job you want—heck, you can work around the clock! This is your life now, old boy. You're a driver, and now you'll be driving all day long.*

It was as if I understood my situation perfectly well, but I just couldn't get past the question of *why* I was in it. Why had this happened? Why had it happened to me? I believed that God and my parents watched over me and looked out for me, and yet they had allowed this to happen. Why? Why had I been disciplined this way? Was there some lesson I needed to learn?

I couldn't figure it out, and that made me angry. I knew bad things happened to good people all the time. I knew that millions of people suffered every single day. People who endured worse losses than mine. Life was loss; I understood that. But still—hadn't I already lost the person who meant the most to me in the world? Hadn't I regularly visited her at the cemetery for the past forty years? If there was some lesson I still needed to learn, some rebuke I still had to accept, did I have to learn and accept it at the expense of Oliver? Was there really no other way?

"God, I just don't get it!" I screamed under the rumble of a Boeing 757 taking off. "I'm trying, but I just don't get it. Please, please, tell me—why is this happening to me?"

And then I was done. *Enough, enough*, I thought. I took a deep breath, straightened my tie, and got in my SUV. Not much later, my client's plane touched down, and I drove him to his home in Mount Kisco. From there I went straight to my third job of the day—picking up a regular client's niece and driving her to Bard College at Simon's Rock in southern Massachusetts.

When I turned seventeen and had to pick a college, I picked a school in upstate New York: SUNY Brockport, a state university ten miles from the northernmost border and nearly four hundred miles from our home on Long Island. I chose it because it was a solid eight-hour drive, which guaranteed minimal visits back home and therefore less time spent with my father.

I know it sounds cruel that I deliberately picked a school so far away in order to escape my father, but living with him had become too difficult. He was constantly drinking or angry or ranting or all three. I was seventeen, trying to figure out my life and my place in the world, and my father wasn't capable of being someone I could turn to for guidance. I loved him, and I felt bad that I'd be leaving him all alone at home. But I truly felt I had no other choice.

To me, it was not my father we all wanted to get away from. It was the disease of alcoholism.

When I was accepted to SUNY Brockport, my father surprised me by saying he wanted to see the school for himself. I'd gone through the application process on my own, and I figured he had no interest in where I went. But all of a sudden, he announced that he would need to provide his solemn approval of my choice.

"I don't care where you're going," he said. "I want to see the school in person before I send you away."

"But, Dad, it's like four hundred miles away. It's up by Buffalo!"

"I don't care if it's in Canada. I'm seeing the school before you go."

There was no preparation for our trip. No calling the school or sending away for information or anything like that. My father and I climbed into his huge 1965 Chrysler Newport, brought along a Hagstrom map, and at 5:00 a.m. one summer morning, set off for northern New York State. The drive itself wasn't too bad. My father often took us children on drives, and these were some of our best times with him. He rarely drank when we went on trips, so our time together in cars—other than my driving lessons—was usually okay.

Plus, out of all the kids, I was my father's favorite travel sidekick and map negotiator—his "navigator," as he called me. He liked having me up in the front of the car with him. It struck me that by insisting we both visit SUNY Brockport, my father had engineered one last long drive together, him at the wheel, me on the map, which I found quite touching. He would never come right out and say he wanted us to spend time together before I left. But I understood that his blunt declaration about needing to see my college was as close as he could get to expressing those feelings. So there we were, Abbott and Costello, out on another long road adventure.

The first six hours passed fairly quickly, or at least they did for me. But after that my father began to get antsy.

"Where the hell is this place?" he muttered under his breath for the final two hours.

When we finally arrived on the campus of SUNY Brockport, neither of us had any idea where to go. My father picked the tallest building and drove toward it. Luckily, it turned out to be the Allen Administration Building. Dad parked right in front of it, in an area that was clearly not for parking.

"Uh, Dad, I don't think we can park here," I said.

"Yes, we can," he said. "I'm not getting out. Just go inside, do what you have to do, and come back."

"What do you mean? You don't want to go inside and see the school for yourself?"

"I don't give a crap what's inside. Just go in, get what you need, and we'll discuss it in the car. Now get out!"

I went into the building and grabbed a few pamphlets and brochures. Then I went back to the Chrysler.

"Well, what do you think?" my father asked.

"I haven't read any of this stuff, but it looks good. What do you think, Dad?"

My father lit a cigarette and looked around.

"I like it. Looks nice. Now let's go."

"That's it? We're going home? Shouldn't we walk around and see the campus?"

"You'll see the campus when you go here. Damn trip is eight hours. Let's get the hell out of here."

And that was that. We stopped once for lunch on the way home and made it back by midnight. My father wasn't trying to be mean or difficult. He just didn't have much patience for anyone or anything. Deep down he loved us all, and he worked really hard to support us. He just didn't take much joy from any of it. He could turn a potentially tender moment of connection into the opposite—a dour moment of estrangement. I never hated my father for the way he was. I just felt sorry for him.

Not surprisingly, I wasn't at all prepared for college life. For instance, I didn't line up a meal plan for myself, nor did I sign up for any classes. I didn't know I had to. I showed up at SUNY Brockport with some clothes, my Sony boom box, a few cassettes, an electric coffeepot, and a small photo of my mother. I had no idea what to expect or what to do.

My first day on campus, I met my new roommate, a great guy named Roger. He asked me what classes I was taking, and he was shocked when I said I didn't know.

"When do I find out?" I asked. "Does someone call me?"

"Steven, no one calls you. You should have already enrolled in them. Classes start in two days."

"Two days? Really? What should I do?"

"You better get to the auditorium right now and sign up," he said, his face a mixture of bafflement and concern.

Not having a meal plan was a big problem too. Every other student had one, it seemed, and I watched them stream into the dining hall to eat lunch and dinner. I learned I needed a plan when I tried to get into the dining hall my second night.

"You have to go to the administration building and get a card," a nice hall staffer told me. "Then you can eat tomorrow."

Great, I thought, *but what do I eat tonight?* I'd already torn through the Funny Bones snack cakes and cookies I'd brought along on my first day on campus, and on this second day, I hadn't eaten a thing. By evening, I was starving. My goal was to make a good impression on my new classmates, so going around asking them for food was out of the question. That wouldn't exactly be the best way to make people think I was cool. Instead, I resigned myself to going hungry—until I remembered I'd packed a single can of Campbell's Chunky soup and a can opener.

I'm saved! I thought, but my joy was premature. I had no way to cook the soup.

And then—an idea. I could cook the soup in my electric coffeepot. Heat is heat, right? I plugged in the pot, dumped in the soup, and went to the bathroom while it warmed up.

When I came out just a few seconds later, the coffeepot was smoking and sputtering. An awful burning smell filled the room. At that precise moment, my roommate returned with several new friends he'd made.

"Oh, hey guys, what's up?" I stammered, trying to wave away the smoke and explain away the dreadful situation. "Well, you see, I have no meal plan, and I'm starving, so I thought I'd just whip up some soup in the coffeepot, that's all."

"This is your roommate?" I heard one of Roger's cool new friends ask him incredulously. "Good luck."

Roger and the rest of them hurried away, leaving me to my smoke and my charred Chunky soup.

Chapter Thirteen

I pulled up to my client Bryce's home in Bedford just after 7:00 p.m. That gave me another half hour to sit and think. From the car I could see a magnificent clock standing in the meadow across from Bryce's home, on the corner of Guard Hill Road and Succabone Road: the Sutton Clock Tower, which is maintained by the Bedford Historical Society. James F. Sutton, the New York City art dealer who built the clock in the late 1880s, did so because his wife, Florence, was homesick for the sound of church bells. He constructed the clock in his barn and connected it to a 550-pound bell. When the barn burned down, neighbors rescued the clock and bell, then chipped in to build the elegant brick tower that now houses the clock. Each year, a group of twelve families become the official Clock Winders who take turns winding it once a month.

I drove by the Sutton Clock Tower often, and I always paused to appreciate its grandeur and endurance. While I was admiring it from my car, it occurred to me that though I'd driven past it probably a hundred times, I'd never once heard it chime. Not a single time. I was sure the sound of the bell would only make me love the old clock more.

At 7:30 p.m., I knocked on Bryce's front door, and he led me into the kitchen. His niece, Isabela Dunlap, whom I'd never met, joined us there. She had long reddish hair and a warm, kind demeanor.

"I heard about Oliver," Bryce said to me. "I'm so sorry."

"What?" Isabela said. "Who's Oliver?"

Bryce explained how he'd seen the News 12 report and how my dog had been stolen four days earlier. Isabela cringed. I could tell she felt bad for me, which made me feel really bad about the whole thing.

"I'm so sorry," she said. "Are you okay to drive?"

"I'm fine," I said. "It's good for me to drive. It takes my mind off the whole Oliver situation."

Bryce kindly suggested we take his Jeep so I could spare my car the mileage. Isabela and I climbed into the car. Isabela asked if she could sit in the front passenger seat, which almost none of my clients do, but it wound up putting us both a little more at ease. Even so, she seemed unsure of what to say to me as we began the eighty-mile drive up Interstate 684, on the way to Route 22 and the town of Great Barrington, Massachusetts. A light snow began to fall, and I flicked on the wipers. For fifteen minutes, we drove in silence.

"Hey, do you mind if we put some music on?" Isabela asked. She held up her phone so I could connect it to the car stereo. I hadn't listened to any music since Oliver disappeared. I'd tried to, but I found I couldn't bear it.

I'm passionate about music. Some songs aren't just songs to me; they're touchstones in my life. I once told my sister Laura that during a particularly difficult period, music saved my life. "Oh, you're exaggerating," she said. But I don't think I was. The things in my life that mattered to me—family, friends, music, Oliver—mattered greatly. I depended on them, and I couldn't afford to lose them. But then I lost Oliver, and when I did, I felt like I lost nearly everything else. What remained would only remind me of what was missing.

My beloved music no longer soothed me. Instead, it would trigger the overwhelming sadness and anger that were always just beneath the surface.

I was afraid that if a song I loved came over the stereo, I would lose it, and I didn't want to lose it in front of Isabela.

Then I thought, *Wait. She's eighteen years old. What are the chances she likes the same music you do? After all, you're stuck in the 1950s and '60s. Surely Isabela listens to music that is slightly more modern than that.*

"Of course," I said, activating the Bluetooth that connected Isabela's phone to the Jeep. I held my breath while the first song cued up. Finally it came on.

It was a song by the Eagles.

Okay, the Eagles are a little retro for an eighteen-year-old, but still, you're okay, Steven. You're safe with the Eagles.

The next song was by the Rolling Stones. The one after that was by the Beatles.

Now we're getting kind of close to the danger line, I thought. *What if Elvis is next? You won't be able to handle it if she plays Elvis.*

"Wow, you have great taste in music," I said.

"Thanks! I love the older stuff because it's what my father listens to."

Oh, great.

The next song was "Burning Love."

"You like Elvis?" I asked, trying to keep my emotions in check and finding it incredulous that an eighteen-year-old could be into my favorite musical artist of all time, a man who died nearly twenty-five years before she was born.

"Oh, I *love* Elvis," she said.

"Yeah, me too. He's my favorite ever. It's just . . . I haven't been able to listen to Elvis since Oliver disappeared."

After a pause, Isabela said, "Do you want me to turn it off? We can turn it off."

"No, leave it. That's okay. I can listen to this. I'm okay."

The next two songs were by Elvis too. The third one was "Always on My Mind." I made it as far as the lyric "Maybe I didn't treat you quite as good as I should have."

Then I felt myself begin to shake. I couldn't stop it. The emotion of the song, the sense of pain and loss in its lyrics, the deep yearning in Elvis's voice—it all tore away at me. Ripped me to pieces. I was crying, then gasping for breath. I was hysterical. Slowly I pulled the car over to the side of the road and apologized.

"I'm sorry," I said. "I just . . . I can't listen to this. It's too hard. I'm so sorry."

I felt Isabela put her hand on my shoulder. She didn't say anything. She just kept her hand there while I wept. After a minute, she handed me a tissue. I felt like I needed to explain why I was so emotional.

"It's just . . . it's just that I don't know if . . ."

I searched and struggled for the right words.

"It's just that I don't know if I told him I loved him that day."

"Oliver knows that you love him," Isabela said.

"Yeah, but I don't know if I *told* him. What if I didn't tell him? I didn't know I would never see him again."

We fell into a silence, and I asked if it was okay if we went to a gas station to get some coffee. I knew I needed to pull myself together. The coffee helped, and we got back on the road. The snow had picked up, but not to the point where it was a problem. In fact, the snow gave the night a wonderfully surreal winter feel, which, under normal circumstances, I would have enjoyed.

"You really love your dog," Isabela said.

It was as if she sensed I needed to talk to someone, which was true—I did. Since Oliver's disappearance, I really hadn't talked about Oliver with anyone, except for my brief conversation with the TV reporter Lisa Reyes. Every moment of every day had been devoted to finding Oliver, not to remembering what he was like or what was special about him. Somehow, Isabela knew that I needed to talk about my boy.

"I do," I replied. "I really do love him. And I'm trying to understand why this happened, you know? To understand why he was taken from me."

"You know, you might get him back. Just because he was taken doesn't mean he was taken forever."

"It's been four days, and we're nowhere," I said. "I'm starting to think God has some lesson he needs to teach me, and I just wish he didn't have to take my dog to show me what it is."

And *just then*, without Isabela saying a word, with the soft snow washing gently across my windshield, it suddenly occurred to me what that lesson might be.

"Maybe it's about love," I went on. "I mean, the outpouring of love I've received since Oliver was taken. Maybe God or my parents are trying to open my eyes to all the love I never realized was there, you know?"

I kept going, believing I was onto something.

"I mean, the person who took Oliver . . . it was an evil act. I hate the act . . . but I don't hate the person. In fact, I refuse to hate that person. Whoever it is just doesn't understand the love that is there between Oliver and me. Doesn't know how that love was created; doesn't know what it means. And I can't judge that person because I don't know how they grew up. I don't know what compelled them to do this. Maybe they never learned to look at a dog as anything but a commodity. As if stealing Oliver were like stealing a cell phone or a purse, and not this little being that I love so much. Whoever took him doesn't realize that what they stole from me was *my life*. It's misguided. This is like a misunderstanding. Whoever took Oliver just doesn't understand the power of that love."

I'd never voiced these ideas before. I'd never even had them, not even as vague thoughts. This all just poured out of me, and when it did, I felt physically and emotionally drained, but not in a bad way. It was like Isabela had relieved me of an enormous burden that had been crushing my chest, simply by giving me the chance to talk.

"Steven, that is beautiful," Isabela finally said. "That is what you have to hold on to. And that is what is going to bring Oliver back to you. Hate can't do it. Only love will. So just hold on to that love."

I was astonished. Who was this teenager to be expressing such a profound sentiment? How could she be so emotionally mature, so eminently wise? I thought of what Isabela said about love, and it brought to mind my favorite Martin Luther King Jr. quote—"Darkness cannot drive out darkness; only light can do that. Hate cannot drive out hate; only love can do that"—and I said it aloud to Isabela, to show her that I understood her message to me.

"That's weird," she said. "That very quote is on a big sign at the entrance to my college."

We arrived at Bard after two hours on the road. I helped Isabela with her bags and told her to be careful not to slip in the snow. Before she left, she looked at me and smiled.

"Steven, you're going to get your dog back. Believe it."

"I will," I told her. "And thank you."

The snow was still tumbling in a steady but harmless way, and I found that on my drive back home, I felt better than I had in days. Something had changed. Unburdening my soul like that focused me on something other than my anger and resentment. Maybe this was about forgiveness. Maybe that was what I needed to focus on. Forgiving my mother and father, whom I'd said so many mean things about in the frustration of this loss. Forgiving whoever took Oliver from me. Forgiving God, as if God needed to be forgiven for anything. Yes, maybe it was about forgiveness—forgiveness and love. Maybe that was the lesson I needed to learn. It still didn't make all that much sense to me, but at least the pieces were beginning to fit together a little better.

Focus on love. Approach the search for Oliver with love, and you will be all right, I thought. *Maybe God is showing you how to be a better human.*

Before I knew it, I was back in Bedford and parked in front of Bryce's home. I put the keys to the Jeep in the cup holder and walked across the driveway to my car. Before I could get in, I heard a sound that stopped me in my tracks.

A chime.

Twelve chimes in all. The Sutton Clock Tower bell was striking midnight.

I stood there in the falling snow and listened to the chimes. They were so pure, so beautiful, so comforting. I stood there and let the sounds wash over me, my breath frosting in the night air, my heart filling with every toll. What did this mean? What was happening? I didn't know for sure, but the feeling I got was that these beautiful chimes served to connect this lovely small town and turn a collection of homes and people into a real community. *We are a community*, I thought. *That's what we humans do. We commune with one another. We help one another. We support one another. We share love.*

I'd never thought of myself as part of a community because I didn't believe I fit in anywhere. But maybe I was wrong. Maybe I was part of something bigger than me.

The last chime sounded. Its fading echo floated around me like the playful snow. As Presidents' Day turned into Tuesday, I felt something very close to hope. Then I got in my car and drove down Guard Hill Road, heading home.

Chapter Fourteen

Around the time I was picking up Isabela on Monday evening, Janice Connolly was settling in to watch TV.

Janice is the kind of friendly, down-to-earth person you could sit and watch a ball game with. Earlier that day, she had returned to her home in Mount Vernon, twenty miles north of New York City, after a three-day-long dog-sitting job in Mahopac, a town farther upstate. For more than twenty years, Janice had been the office manager for a veterinary technician at a Yonkers animal clinic, and she also worked at an animal shelter. But the clinic had closed three years ago, and now Janice worked part-time for a pet groomer. She was happy to be home from Mahopac, and after having dinner with her husband, Derek, she sat on her comfortable teal-green sofa and turned on the evening news. Her two shorthair cats—tortoise-colored Ming and jet-black Ling—jumped up on the sofa with her.

She switched the channel to News 12 Westchester, her favorite news show, which she watched every morning and every evening. Nothing on the night's newscast grabbed her attention until the reporter Lisa Reyes came on and showed a clip of a dog being chased around a driveway by a cat.

That's funny, she thought. *A cat chasing a dog.*

By the time her head hit her pillow that night, Janice had forgotten all about the silly dog on TV.

The next morning, Janice got up at six thirty and went to buy groceries at the North Food Store. Janice lived in a four-story, redbrick building on Norton Street, next to a vacant lot and a mechanic's shop. The block was half-residential, half-industrial, in an area that had seen better days. But Janice liked living there because it was a real neighborhood—people looked out for each other. Like her husband, Derek, Janice was born and raised in nearby Yonkers, and Mount Vernon felt like home to her. Norton Street had its own character, its own charm. It was a family block, a place full of friendly, caring people.

Janice walked out of the building and came down the five-step stoop. She noticed a white Subaru Forester SUV parked in front of the building, and she recognized the young man behind the wheel. His name was Del, and Janice had heard talk of his reputation in the area as a troublemaker. In Janice's mind, he was someone who hadn't received much guidance in his life and sorely needed it. She went over to the white SUV to say hello.

"What are you doing out so early, Del?" Janice asked.

"My mom won't let me in the house with the dog," he said.

Janice looked down and saw the dog. It was a little thing, curled up in a dog bed on the passenger seat. The dog looked up at Janice with big, timid eyes, and Janice thought, *Oh my goodness, he's so adorable*. She wondered where Del had gotten it, but she knew enough not to ask.

"Do you know anyone who wants a dog?" Del asked.

"I don't know, maybe," Janice said. "Let me take a picture."

Janice snapped a photo of the dog and asked Del for his phone number so she could call him in case she found a taker. Then she left to catch her Metro-North train on her way to her job at the groomer's. When she got to the store, Janice asked the groomer if she knew anyone who might want the dog.

"I *do* know someone who is looking for a small dog," the groomer said.

Janice called Del to let him know.

"Okay," Del said. "I want two hundred fifty dollars for the dog."

Janice was surprised, though she quickly realized she shouldn't have been. This was Del, after all. Always working an angle. She explained to him that no one would pay him for the dog—this was about finding the dog a good, safe home. Del insisted on the payment.

"Okay, well, good luck then," Janice said, and she hung up.

A little while later, a customer came into the store with her dog. "He needs a bath and grooming," the customer said. Janice took the little dog to the tiled basin, turned on the faucet, and tested the water to make sure it was warm. She was glad to see the dog didn't mind getting wet—he even seemed to enjoy the process.

"Good boy," Janice told him as she lathered him up with shampoo. "Such a good boy."

The dog was a little black-and-brown Yorkie terrier. Janice, who'd owned and loved many dogs and cats over the years, was impressed by the Yorkie's friendly demeanor. She knew some Yorkies could be snappy and high-strung, but not this one. This one was docile and loving.

Come to think of it, Janice thought, *so was the dog in Del's white SUV*. That dog looked like a Yorkie, too, and had also seemed like a sweetheart. *How about that*, she thought. *Two sweet little Yorkies in one morning.*

Then it hit her.

The dog in the white SUV—it had looked strangely familiar. She felt as though she had seen him before . . . somewhere.

And she had. The dog on TV. The cute little dog being chased by a cat. The news report about a stolen dog in nearby Scarsdale. Was that the same dog in the SUV? Was that the dog everyone was looking for?

Or was it just a weird coincidence?

Janice went back to shampooing the Yorkie in the basin.

The Search: Day Five
February 19

Oliver doesn't like it when I talk on the phone. He takes it as an affront of some kind. If I pick up the phone, Oliver will turn his back to me and wander away, and if it's summertime and the cottage door is open, he'll wander out into the field. It's as if he's saying, Okay, fine, if you're not going to pay me any mind, I'll just go and talk to the cows and sheep then.

Oliver gets along pretty well with the other animals on the farm. Some of them, I believe, are fond of him, but certainly they all tolerate him. Oliver likes it when I grab a loaf of bread off the top of my fridge and go out to feed the goats. He follows along and gets in line and waits for his turn. One time, he got a little too close to the goats, and one of them put its head down and gave him a good little shove. Oliver got the message pretty quickly. Now he never, ever tries to cut the line.

It makes me happy to see Oliver out in the fields with the goats and sheep and cows and rabbits. It's funny to see them get along so well—even tiny Oliver and the big white horse named Po. They're all wildly different, and yet, when you think about it, they're all basically the same.

Chapter Fifteen

On Monday night I decided not to stay at Laura's house and instead slept in an extra bedroom at Lucy's house in Bedford. It was my first night's sleep in a bed, not on a sofa, in five days. I still couldn't bear to be in my own cottage without Oliver there, but at least I'd made it back to Lucy's place, which was *near* my cottage. That was progress.

When I woke up at six o'clock in the morning, I still felt good from the night before—from my conversation with Isabela and from my midnight moment at the Sutton Clock Tower. I knew I'd made some kind of breakthrough in my attitude and approach to losing Oliver, and that felt significant. At the same time, it had been four full days and I still didn't have Oliver. I still didn't have a single clue as to where he was. I wasn't going to stop looking for Oliver—not any time soon, maybe not ever. But even so, I had to begin preparing myself for never seeing him again. I had to accept that this was possible, or even probable. And accepting that was the hardest thing I'd ever have to do.

Before the old feelings of anger and resentment came rushing back, I decided I wanted to somehow capture the wave of love and acceptance that had washed over me the night before. I felt like I needed to make my thoughts known. And I knew that I wanted to do it on my own Facebook page.

As I said, I wasn't much of a Facebook person. I rarely posted anything beyond a photo of Oliver or of my sisters and me. But now there was an entire post devoted to Oliver, and it was being followed by thousands of people. Thousands! Nancy had handled all the updates so far, but I realized it was time for me to post something on my page, too, to thank everyone for the outpouring of love.

It was time for me to share what was in my heart.

I asked Lucy if I could use the computer in her workroom, and she said go right ahead. I sat at her desk and stared at the blank screen and wondered where to begin. The next hour was a blur, and when it was over, I'd written a long essay titled "I Am Caught in a Storm."

On one side of this storm, my life is destroyed. I can't sleep in my own bed. I can't go to the gym. I can't listen to music. I haven't listened to a song in four days. I can't go for my daily walk because my companion is gone. I can't cook because my buddy isn't there to eat with me. I can barely walk into my cottage to grab a change of clothes. At least I can work, because that's about the only thing I did without him.

On the other side, I'm witnessing the support and love for me and my companion grow every day to monumental proportions! I'm either crying because I miss Oliver or crying because the love I'm feeling from everyone is incredible. I haven't had time to read all the comments, but from what I've read, I see the true spirit of humanity. Inherently, we all want to be good. In times of crisis, we drop all the labels and rise above the meaningless stereotypes and become godlike in our actions.

I'm watching this unfold before my eyes, and it's like witnessing a miracle.

I wrote about how my sisters would do anything to help me. I wrote about how I was a spiritual person who believed his mother and father and brother were looking out for him from beyond. I wrote about how I had memorized some passages of Scripture and how much God's words had touched me. I wrote about the patterns in my life and about the Carino way—one step forward, two steps back. And I spoke directly to Oliver.

I know you are frightened, and I know you miss me, as I do you. But I KNOW that whoever has you right now is loving you because that is all any person could do when they are in your presence. It is IMPOSSIBLE not to love you. My heart is breaking as I write this, but I know I will hold you again, because this person did not mean to destroy us. They just saw your beauty, and they took you for themselves. If you only knew how you are bringing out the very best in everyone, you would be amazed! Hold on, my little boy, and we will go for those walks again soon.

When I was done writing, I put my finger over the RETURN key to post my essay. But I couldn't do it. I couldn't press the key. This was too personal, too honest to share with the world. Did I really want to do this? I sat in the chair for a long time, wondering if I should share the post or delete it.

Just then, my cell phone sounded.

"Hello?"

"Yes, hi, is this Steven?"

"Yes, this is Steven."

"Is your dog missing?"

"Yes, my dog is missing."

"Well, I'm calling about a dog I saw this morning that looks like your dog."

So far I'd received three or four calls from people who believed they'd spotted Oliver in some far-off place—a shelter in Iowa, a shelter in Florida, places like that. I'd asked them to send me photos, and none of the dogs were Oliver. So I wasn't terribly hopeful about this latest call.

"Okay, well, where did you see him?"

"In Mount Vernon. There's a guy down there, and he offered to sell me this dog for two hundred fifty dollars. And the dog was in a white SUV. I think the dog has been living in that truck."

"How did you get my number?" I asked.

"I looked for it on Facebook after I saw the video with the dog and the cat."

"What video?"

"You know, the cat chasing the dog."

I wasn't aware that News 12 had run another report, this one featuring the video Laura had sent them, the one from my phone. That was news to me. But obviously, this person had seen it, and now she believed she'd seen Oliver.

"I think this guy who has him has been in and out of trouble," she continued. "I took the dog's picture in case I found someone who wanted the dog."

"You have a photo? Can you send it to me?"

The woman hesitated. She explained she was calling me from someone else's phone and could send me the photo later. My guess was that she was being cautious and didn't want the person who had the dog to ever know she was the one who called me. Maybe she knew him; maybe she lived near him. Maybe he was a dangerous person.

"Okay, okay," I said. "Would you please send me the photo as soon as you can? I really need to see that photo."

"I'll send it to you when I get back to work," she said.

"Where is the dog now? Can you tell me where he is right now?"

"If he's still there, he's at 328 Norton Street in Mount Vernon."

I hung up and realized my hands were shaking. *Wait for the photo,* I told myself. *Don't get all worked up. Not yet. Wait for the photo. Wait to see if it's him.*

Lucy came downstairs and asked me who I'd been talking to. I told her about the dog in the white SUV.

"I'm waiting to see the photo," I said as calmly as I could.

"Well, maybe we should go there now, just in case," Lucy said. "Are you doing anything else?"

In fact, I wasn't doing anything at all. I hadn't made any plans for how to look for Oliver that day. There was no reason I couldn't get up and drive to Mount Vernon on the outside chance the dog in the SUV was Oliver.

"Okay," I told Lucy, "I'll do it. I'll go there now."

"I'm coming with you," Lucy said.

"Okay, fine. Just let me do one thing before we go."

I went back to Lucy's computer and looked over what I'd written one last time. Then I hit the key to post it and went upstairs to get ready to go to Mount Vernon.

Chapter Sixteen

From the car I phoned Laura and told her about the call. She got a lot more excited about it than I had been. She said she wasn't too far from Mount Vernon and would drive there immediately and buy the dog for $250 before anyone else could get him. I told her not to go. I'd driven through Mount Vernon many times. I knew there were a few parts of town that were a little suspect, and I didn't want Laura walking around there asking about a man in a white SUV.

"Besides, we don't know if it's Oliver," I said. "I'm waiting for the photo. Just wait for us, and we'll pick you up soon."

Normally, Laura would have argued with me, and at the end of the argument, she would have put her foot down and gone to Mount Vernon anyway. But this time she deferred to my wishes. After our talk about how I sometimes didn't appreciate her bossiness, I think she decided to just let me have my way. It actually felt kind of strange.

A few minutes later, I got an alert on my cell. It was from a blocked cell-phone number. I opened the text and saw it was a photo. I was almost too nervous to look at it. What if it wasn't Oliver? Had I gotten my hopes up despite trying so hard not to? How would I react if it wasn't him?

I took a deep breath and looked at the photo of the dog, who was curled up in a square bed in the passenger seat of an SUV. Then I nearly drove off the Hutchinson River Parkway.

"It's him!" I said.

"What?" Lucy said.

"The picture. It's him! It's Oliver!"

I handed the phone to Lucy and asked, "Is it him?"

"It looks like him."

"I know, but is it him?"

"Oh my God, it *is* him."

"It is him, right? It's Oliver. But is it really him?" I asked again.

"Steven, it's him. Look at him. That's Oliver!"

"I know, that's Oliver. That dog is Oliver! But is it really him?"

I didn't know how to react. Cautiously? Joyously? I knew it was Oliver in the photo. I knew it the instant I saw it. The way he was curled up, the way he looked up at the camera, his ears, his little nose, his serene demeanor—that was Oliver. And he was acting just like I knew he would—he was playing it cool. Part of me, though, could hardly believe it was him. Was it possible that I could be on the verge of getting Oliver back? Would that kind of miraculous outcome ever happen to me?

"I'm calling the Mount Vernon Police Department," I told Lucy. "We need them there when we approach this guy."

I got through to the police station and told the desk sergeant about Oliver. I told him exactly where Oliver was and how they had to hurry up and get him before this guy in the Subaru took off.

"Okay, we'll send someone out," the sergeant said.

Then I called Laura and told her we were five minutes from her house.

"Be ready to jump in the car," I said. "It's Oliver. It's him in the photo. He's in Mount Vernon."

Laura was waiting in her driveway when we pulled up. She got in, and I drove down the Bronx River Parkway as fast as I could, careful not to speed too much. It took us twenty minutes to arrive in Mount Vernon. The GPS steered us toward Norton Street.

When I turned the corner onto the street, I almost couldn't breathe. It was all too much. The possibility that Oliver was there. The possibility that he wasn't. I held the steering wheel tightly and slowly worked my way down the block, looking for the mysterious white Subaru.

Then I saw it. It was right where the caller had told me it was—in the middle of the block, outside 328 Norton Street. A white Subaru Forester. I pulled my car to the curb and jumped out and ran toward the SUV. There was no one in the driver's seat, but I didn't care—all I cared about was Oliver. I ran around to the passenger side and looked through the window.

"Oliver!" I yelled out.

But he wasn't there. The seat was empty. I looked through all the windows, and Oliver wasn't anywhere.

Just then, I noticed the two young uniformed police officers standing behind the white SUV.

Laura came up behind me. She saw my expression and turned to the cops.

"Where's the dog?" she asked.

"What dog?" one of the officers said.

"My brother's dog. He was in the car. Somebody took him, and he was in this car."

"We didn't see any dog here, lady."

"What are you talking about?" I said. "He was here! He was right here just a while ago."

"We don't know about any dog," the cop said. "All we know is we ran these plates, and this car is stolen. But we never saw a dog."

Here it was again—the Carino Curse. The SUV was there, but Oliver wasn't. Of course he wasn't. I'd warned myself not to get my hopes up, and yet I had. I'd fully expected to see Oliver sitting in that passenger seat. What was I thinking? Why would I have ignored my own past history? Didn't I know the Carino Curse was patient and persistent? That it would give me a little and then always snatch it away?

For a while in my life, I thought I might be able to conquer the curse. Back in college, I survived the embarrassing soup-in-the-coffee-pot incident and made it through all four years at SUNY Brockport, though for most of that time I was lonely and unhappy. There were, however, a few memorable moments and happy times. For instance, I somehow found the courage to walk into the college radio station, WBSU, and persuade them to give me my own radio show on Sunday nights from nine to twelve. I'd take requests from callers (who were usually Nancy and her friends), and I'd play the Go-Go's or Joan Jett or whoever they wanted to hear. When my roommate and his buddies got over my infamous coffeepot mishap, they even asked me to play records at their Halloween dorm party. My sister Nancy came to the party, and I could tell she was happy for me. I was never more in my element than when I was spinning those records.

I graduated with a BS in history and a concentration in—big surprise—American history. I had a B average, which was decent, and a B-plus in my concentration. Mostly, though, I was relieved to be through with college—even if meant temporarily moving back to Long Island and living with my father again. To keep busy while I figured out what my career would be, I took a job as a driver for a courier company for $5.50 an hour. I expected my father to denigrate my choice of jobs, but by then he wasn't his usual gruff self. He was still occasionally ornery, but he was suffering from emphysema, even while he continued to drink and smoke. He was often weak and subdued, like a wounded old bear. I watched his health deteriorate a little more each day.

In my late twenties, I met a woman, fell in love, and got married. Actually, I don't think either of us was truly in love with the other. I remember thinking while we were dating that I wanted to break up with her, but I didn't have the guts to do it. In the end, it was just easier to marry her. I ignored all the warning signs and went through with the wedding, setting myself up for the inevitable pain of a disintegrating marriage.

In the meantime, I threw myself into my work. I started an employment/consulting agency called Rhino Resources, put together a roster of twenty-five or so computer consultants, and hired them out to the likes of J. P. Morgan and Citibank to help the banks set up their computer networks. To my surprise, the business was successful. The demand for computer help seemed endless, and the money poured in. I got myself a Mercedes-Benz, a gold Cartier watch, and a few Armani suits, and my wife and I moved into a $500,000 home in New Rochelle. By any objective measure, good old Steven Carino was doing pretty well.

Of course, it didn't last. One day I came home from the office and told my wife I didn't think our relationship was working. She agreed, and just like that, after four years, our marriage was over.

My business went next. As banks and other companies began to staff their own tech experts, the need for consultants dwindled. My roster shrank from a high of thirty consultants to just a handful. I wasn't as crushed by the downturn as I might have been because, by then, I wanted to quit the business anyway. I was tired of all the stress and anxiety. Plus, I had a nice sum of money in the bank, certainly enough to tide me over until I figured out my next move. Without much fanfare, Rhino Resources simply ceased to be.

That's when the Carino Curse kicked in.

I had started drinking in college, when drowning my misery in a few cans of beer was how most of my evenings ended. The booze would loosen me up enough to allow me to interact with people in a reasonably normal way. Without beer, I had absolutely no chance of talking to a girl I didn't know, much less impressing her or asking her for a date. With a few beers under my belt, I became much more social and likable, even garrulous. I believed I needed to drink to resemble a regular human being.

The downside to drinking happened when I got home. That was when I'd be alone and drink more beers and begin to beat myself up. *What a loser you are*, I'd say to myself. *Here you are, all alone again, drinking by yourself. What a loser.* I'd drink until I passed out, and I'd wake up with a crippling hangover. Then I'd start the cycle all over again—a few beers before going out, more beers while I was out, a few more when I got home. I was never hostile after I drank, like my father could be, except if you count being hostile to myself.

I stopped drinking altogether during my marriage, but once it was over, I went back to my old ways. I graduated from beer to red wine, and to loosen up before a night out, I'd drink a whole bottle on my own. I'm not sure I ever spoke to a woman sober during that period of my life. I always needed a drink—several drinks, actually—in order to pass myself off as a confident, normal man.

When my business went under, my drinking got worse. I never

did anything too destructive on my nights of drinking, like drive a car or turn over a table or anything like that. Instead, I went home, drank another bottle or two, and berated myself like my father had berated me all my life. All along I knew I was in some kind of trouble, but I didn't know what to do about it. I didn't want to stop drinking because that would mean the end of my social life. At the same time, I *did* want to stop drinking because I hated how self-critical I became at the end of the night. It was almost as if I needed someone else to make the decision for me; I couldn't make it on my own.

That scenario finally happened on Saint Patrick's Day. I'd recently closed my business, and I was living alone and feeling more miserable than ever. I knew most of my friends and colleagues celebrated the day with each other at happy parties, but I had no interest in joining them. Instead, I went to the liquor store, bought two bottles of red wine and a fifth of Jack Daniel's, and went back home for a party of my own.

In my one-bedroom Manhattan apartment on 23rd Street and Sixth Avenue, I turned on the TV to a channel that played transcendental music. It was peaceful music, and that was what I needed more than anything: some inner peace. I sat in my rocking chair and popped open the first bottle of red. It didn't take long for me to empty both bottles of wine. Then I turned my attention to the fifth of Jack Daniel's that was sitting on the kitchen counter, just waiting for me.

In that moment I recognized the full reality of my situation, and I said it aloud to myself.

"Steven, if you open that bottle of Jack, you're going to die tonight."

I got up from my chair and wobbled into the kitchen. I hadn't been as intensely confused and unhappy since the day my mother passed away. I grabbed the edge of the counter to steady myself and stared down at the bottle. I didn't want to stop drinking because then, eventually, I'd get sober, and sober Steven had nothing to offer the world, whereas drunk Steven did. So why not keep drinking? Why not play Russian roulette? What did I have to lose? I took the bottle in one hand and screwed off the cap with the other. The smell of the whiskey hit my nose.

"Here goes," I said.

Then I poured the whole bottle into the sink.

I left the empty bottle on the counter because I wanted whoever found me to think I had drunk it all. I wanted someone to figure out that I had a problem and begin the process of solving it, which was something I couldn't do. I called my good friend Jesse, and luckily he picked up.

"I need help," I said. "I think I'm going to die tonight."

I put down the phone and lay across my sofa. I don't know how much time passed, but before long there was a hard pounding on the door. It was the building doorman. Finally he used his key and rushed in. Two paramedics with a stretcher followed behind. I woke up the next morning in a hospital bed with a tube down my throat. I spent the next two days in the hospital, and four more after that at the Cabrini Medical Center, getting the toxins out of my body. I hadn't cried for help; I'd *screamed* for help. And my call was answered.

Back on Norton Street in Mount Vernon, Laura lost her cool with the police. The officers were nice enough, but they weren't interested in anything other than the stolen car. When they told us they had to tow the car to the pound, Laura was indignant.

"You can't take the car!" she said. "My brother's dog was in the car, and whoever has him won't come back if you tow the car away. You have to leave the car here."

"We're sorry, lady. We have to take the car. It's stolen."

"You cannot take this car!"

One of the cops gave me a look that I interpreted as *Rein her in a little, okay?*

"Laurie, hold on, you're talking to the cops here," I said, standing between her and the officers. The last thing I needed was my sister ending up in a holding cell.

Eventually I got Laura to calm down, and I calmed down myself too. I had no choice but to take this setback in stride.

"Look, we'll keep an eye out for your dog," one of the officers said. "But be careful out here. Watch your back."

I took one last look into the SUV, just to be sure. It was empty, just as it had been before. Oliver wasn't there. Oliver was gone again.

But maybe, just maybe, he wasn't too far away.

Chapter Seventeen

It wasn't lost on me that my search for Oliver had led me to a place called Mount Vernon—named for the Virginia plantation of George Washington. The area had been the scene of several Revolutionary War battles, inspiring the people who settled there in the 1850s to give it its presidential name. Now, the boy who knew all the presidents was there, trying to find his dog.

Mount Vernon is not a small town. With nearly seventy thousand residents, it's the eighth most populous city in New York State. Plenty of famous people grew up there—Dick Clark, Denzel Washington, Art Carney. The Brooklyn Dodger who gave up Bobby Thomson's famous "Shot Heard Round the World" home run, Ralph Branca, was raised there. Tucked between the Bronx and Hutchinson Rivers, Mount Vernon—and especially its North Side, where we were—is one of the most ethnically diverse cities in the county. Whites, Blacks, Latinos, Asians, Native Americans, Brazilians, and others share its streets. Part of the city is home to million-dollar homes. Other parts are mainly apartments and split-family dwellings. There is a little bit of everything in Mount Vernon; it's a hard city to characterize in any uniform way.

All that mattered about Mount Vernon to us, though, was that, with any luck, Oliver was somewhere in it.

While we were talking to the police officers, my cell phone sounded. My friend Tony Marcogliese was calling. He's a colorful character who works in the garbage business, and I'd known him for about eight years. We met through a mutual friend and got along pretty well. When Tony tore up his foot and was laid up in a hospital in Valhalla, I went to see him a couple of times to cheer him up—something he was hugely grateful for and never forgot. When I was down on my luck and scraping out a living by driving a limo, Tony would hire me to take him into New York City and would hand me a hundred-dollar bill, at least double the fare. We didn't talk or get together all that often, but we had the kind of friendship where we knew we'd be there for each other in difficult times.

And this was a difficult time.

"Steven, I heard about Oliver," Tony said. "I'm so sorry, man. How are you holding up?"

"Tony, I'm in Mount Vernon looking for him! Someone just spotted him a while ago."

"Wait, what? Where are you? I'm coming down."

"You don't have to do that," I said.

"Give me the address, and I'll be right there."

I didn't argue. Tony lived thirty miles away in Pound Ridge. I knew he would come even if I insisted otherwise.

Laura, Lucy, and I stood on Norton Street and watched a police tow truck take away the white SUV. After five days of having no idea where Oliver was, it was breathtaking to know where he'd physically been just a little bit earlier. My Oliver had sat in that very SUV just hours ago. It was almost as if I could still feel him there, which is why it was so hard to watch the police take the SUV away.

On the plus side, we'd narrowed our search area from the entire world to, hopefully, a square mile or so in Mount Vernon. Still, a square mile gives you a whole bunch of places to hide a twelve-pound dog.

"Okay, so what are we going to do?" Lucy asked.

"We have to ask around about Oliver," Laura said. "Someone must have seen him. Let's start over there."

Laura walked to the mechanic shop next to a fenced-in lot. It was a squat two-story brick building with a one-floor extension built behind it. Two men in gray mechanic's outfits were standing outside the shop. One was older and had white whiskers. The other was younger and stocky. Laura went over and showed them Oliver's photo. Then she came running over to me.

"They know something!" she said.

I went over, and together we questioned the men. I guess I expected some resistance, but they were immediately friendly and helpful.

"This kid poked his head in this morning and said he had a cute dog for sale for two hundred fifty dollars," Terry, the older one, told us. "I asked him where the dog was, and he said in the car."

"So you never saw the dog?" I asked.

"No, because we told him we weren't interested," Terry said. "It's funny—my wife and I saw the TV report about a stolen dog last night. You know, with the cat chasing the dog? We were watching it and laughing our butts off. But I didn't realize that was the same dog the kid was selling."

Just like the caller, Terry had made the connection too late.

"Do you know who this kid is?" I asked.

The two men were suddenly quiet. They looked at each other but didn't say a word. Finally, Rolando, the younger of the two mechanics, said, "Yeah, I know him. He wears a baseball cap. He doesn't have a great reputation."

"Do you happen to know where he lives?"

Rolando hesitated again. Then he pointed at the four-story, red-brick building down the street, right where the white SUV had been parked.

"He lives in that building," Rolando said.

Terry and Rolando let us put up flyers outside their shop and promised they'd keep an eye out for the kid and for Oliver. Laura, Lucy, and I regrouped. Now that we knew where the person who took Oliver lived, what were we going to do? Wait for him to come back? Go in and ask around about him? Call the cops again? It was Laura who came up with a plan.

"Lucy and I will go back to my house and print up more flyers," she said. "We need to plaster the area with flyers. Also, give me that lady's phone number. I want to talk to her myself."

I gave Laura the number of the woman who had called about Oliver. If anyone could get more information out of her, it was Laura.

"When Tony gets here, you can ask around and see what else you can find out," Laura said.

Tony showed up just a few minutes later.

Tony isn't the type of guy to make a quiet entrance. He is, to say the least, distinctive. I watched him steer his big black Range Rover down Norton Street and park it across from the redbrick building. I watched as the door opened and Tony stepped out. He was wearing a multicolor fur coat and thick black sunglasses. His dark, graying hair was slicked back like a gangster. He had on a T-shirt, jeans, and huge boots. If you didn't know him, you might think he was trouble. In fact, he was one of the sweetest, most generous men I'd ever known.

"Steven," he said, before wrapping me in a bear hug.

"You didn't have to come down," I said. "I've got people helping me find Oliver."

"Steven, I know how much you love your dog, but I didn't come down here for Oliver," Tony said. "I came down here for you. You're my friend, and I'd do anything for you."

I don't think Tony had any idea how much those words meant to me.

"So let's get to it," Tony said. "Let's find Oliver."

We got in Tony's Range Rover and drove around the block, looking for the kid in a baseball cap. We stopped at a deli at the corner of Norton Street, and I asked the woman behind the counter if she'd seen anyone selling a dog.

"Yes, he was in here this morning," she said. "He was trying to sell me this dog he had in the car."

We got back in the Range Rover and drove back down Norton Street. Rolando, the mechanic, flagged me down.

"Follow me," he said. "I think I may know where your dog is."

My heart pounded in my chest like a drum.

Rolando took us to the vacant lot next to the redbrick building where the kid in the baseball cap lived.

"There's a lady back here who thinks she heard a dog barking," Rolando said.

We went to a little courtyard behind the building. I was running, not walking. A woman in her forties was there. She had two young children with her, neither older than ten. They appeared to be fanning out and looking for Oliver.

"My kids heard a little dog barking in back of the building," the mother explained to me. "So I came back here, but he's not here."

I looked into the courtyard. It was a small, grim place. It might have been a courtyard at one point, but now it looked more like a garbage dump. It was about fifteen feet wide by twenty feet deep and surrounded by a six-foot-tall chain-link fence. The fence was partly torn down and shredded in spots. Only small patches of grass remained, and those were covered with debris—a mattress, old clothes, cans and bottles, a ragged piece of a car bumper. I pulled apart the torn fencing and squeezed into the yard, searching every last inch for Oliver. But by then it was obvious Oliver wasn't there.

"Maybe he's still around here somewhere," Tony said.

"What's his name?" the mother asked.

"Oliver."

She told her young children to walk around and call out Oliver's name. Tony and I called out his name too. We searched the length of the vacant lot to the right of the redbrick building, until we wound up on the avenue behind Norton Street. I looked at the street sign and was struck by the name: Garfield Avenue. Another president.

What is it with all the president stuff? I wondered.

To our right, we saw a sprawling, fenced-in lot filled with construction equipment, red traffic cones, and a big red dump truck. My first thought was, *There's a lot of places for a dog to hide in there.* If whoever took Oliver had put him in the courtyard, and if Oliver had snuck out and walked away, he probably would have looked for a secluded place to lie down. Oliver could be in this lot.

I tried to open the fence door, but it was securely fastened with a thick chain and padlock. The top of the fence was ringed with barbed wire. There was no way in. Nor did we have any idea who owned the lot. We were stuck outside.

"Look there," I said to Tony, pointing to a small gap of about a foot between the bottom of the fence and the concrete pavement. "If we try to lift that a little, I can get in."

Tony squatted and pulled at the bottom of the fence with all his might. It gave another few inches. I got down on my stomach and began to slither under. I was possessed, crawling through the dirt with abandon to somehow get to Oliver. I got stuck several times, but I kept squirming through, my pants and shirt ripping against the concrete, my fingers clawing at the ground to pull me forward. Tony summoned all his strength and gave the fence a mighty tug, and with a final surge I was through. I stood up covered in dust and dirt.

Rolando, the mechanic, had watched the whole thing.

"That is one crazy dude," he said to Tony.

"You don't know how much this dog means to him," Tony replied.

I ran through the lot, calling out Oliver's name, crawling under trucks, pulling at heavy wood pallets, frantically searching every little corner. It took me close to an hour to canvas the lot. By the end of my search, I was sweating, breathing heavily, and black with filth and grime.

And *still*—I didn't find Oliver.

Chapter Eighteen

It all began way, way back—with Michael.

Michael was a medium-sized Yorkshire terrier my sister Nancy brought home when I was nine. I remember we eventually took him over to our aunt Diane's house so she could mate him with her shih tzu. I didn't pay all that much attention to Michael because back then my mother was alive and healthy, and I got all the love and nourishment I needed from her. But less than two years after Michael arrived, my mother was diagnosed with cancer.

After the diagnosis, the level of chaos in our home intensified. My father's alcoholic rages continued, but now we added regular trips to the hospital and endless bottles of painkillers for my mom. The mood in our house became increasingly grim. I have no doubt that the chaos and disruption in our lives affected our pets too. After all, dogs are hugely sensitive to people's moods, and in our house, people's moods were usually pretty dark.

In the middle of it all, my father got laid off from his job. That added another layer of anxiety and insecurity for our family. Then, in late 1974, on the morning of November 4, when Michael was only two years old, he got hit by a car in front of our house. My father wrapped him in a towel, put him in the Ford station wagon, and drove him to the animal hospital. I went along and held Michael in the back seat. He was barely breathing, and blood was running out of his mouth. By the time we got to the hospital, Michael was gone.

We buried Michael, wrapped in that same towel, in the backyard. I marked the grave site with a little stick, and I sat beside it often, unaware of what was drawing me there. I didn't know it at the time, but what I was doing was grieving.

Michael's mating with our aunt's shih tzu produced a litter of six puppies, and I was allowed to pick one out for us to bring home. I chose the last one to be born, and I named her Marcie. Marcie was the first dog I ever truly loved and considered my own. As my mother got sicker, Marcie and I grew closer. I turned to her for the unconditional love and affection I could no longer get from my ailing mother.

Like me, Marcie was sensitive and easily hurt. If she saw my mother suffering through a particularly painful day, Marcie would hide under my mother's bed and stay there until Mom felt better. Marcie would also hide there when my father came home screaming and ranting. The stress of our household affected her—she didn't eat much, she scratched herself a lot, and she needed constant reassurance from me that everything would be okay, the same way I needed constant reassurance from my mother.

Yet, as fragile as she was, Marcie got me through my miserable teenage years. After my mother died, Marcie and I were inseparable. Not only was her love for me clear and profound; she was also always there for me whenever I needed her. And boy, did I need her a lot.

As a teenager, I was a mess. A chubby, pimple-faced, anxiety-ridden mess. After being the smart young boy who did everything right, I was suddenly the weirdo who did everything wrong. There were days when I felt so confused and inferior that I came to hate my very existence. The thing that kept me going was Marcie's unconditional love.

When I turned eighteen, I had to leave for college—and leave Marcie behind. It was one of the hardest things I've ever had to do. I couldn't stand the thought of leaving her all alone in the house with my father, but I had no choice; I couldn't take her with me. Reluctantly, I left without her, and I cried with happiness whenever I traveled back home and saw her again. Marcie was never just a dog or a pet to me. She was, in many ways, the emotional center of my complicated life.

In my sophomore year, my father called me to tell me Marcie had died. She wasn't even nine years old. I knew that my father liked Marcie and took good care of her, but I also knew his angry ravings took a heavy toll on her. Without me there to soothe her and let her know it would be okay, I believe she absorbed all of his sadness and regret. In the end she stopped eating and passed away. My father somehow found a way to blame me for her death.

After college I lived in a little studio apartment in New York City. I worked for an advertising agency, and I had a small circle of friends. I even had a girlfriend, who would later become my wife. I was, at twenty-nine, a reasonable impersonation of a happy, functioning adult, though beneath it all, I was still plagued by self-loathing and an extreme lack of confidence. It's just that I was doing a much better job of hiding it.

On a whim, my then-girlfriend and I walked into a pet store one day, and she immediately suggested I get a dog of my own. "It will help you with your depression," she said. I played along and agreed to sit in the back room of the store with an uncommonly adorable apricot poodle. Whether it was my girlfriend's insistence that the dog would do me good or my own instant connection to the pup, I ended up walking out of the store with a brand-new pet, purchased on a credit card. I was quickly overwhelmed by regret when I realized how long it would take me to pay off that credit card.

Later that day, my girlfriend and I went to a coffee shop and talked about what we should name my pretty little poodle. No name seemed right, until I poured a little milk into my coffee and watched it change into a vaguely apricot color.

"She's Coffee," I announced. "Her name is Coffee."

Coffee changed my life. She banished all my fears. She gave me a sense of purpose and identity that had not been there before. When I walked her around my neighborhood, I couldn't go a block without someone stopping me to play with her and tell me how cute she was. One time, a police car pulled up next to me, and the cop who was driving called out to me. I wondered what I'd done wrong.

"Excuse me," the cop said, "do you mind if we say hello to your dog?"

Coffee became the one essential thing my life could revolve around. Everything else was less important and would eventually fall into place. She filled my dingy little studio with playfulness and joy, and she filled my life with meaning and hope. I became a kind of local celebrity in the neighborhood; as long as I had Coffee, everyone was always delighted to see me. There had been an emptiness in my soul ever since the day my mother passed away. I never imagined that a tiny eight-pound dog could fill that emotional void, but that's just what Coffee did. Getting her was one of the greatest things that had ever happened in my twenty-nine years on earth.

The new perspective Coffee gave me led to good things happening. I got into the field of executive recruiting, got married, and bought a house in New Rochelle. I went from being broke to running a multimillion-dollar consultancy business. On Christmases my wife and I would fill the house with guests, and Coffee and I would dance around the tree. Coffee made me take my life less seriously because everything she did made me laugh. Having Coffee in my life made me feel unstoppable.

It was all like a dream come true—and for me, it was all because of Coffee.

After my marriage ended, Coffee and I moved back to New York City. I took her with me to work every day, and she would sit calmly on my desk and greet any visitors. She gave everyone she met a huge jolt of joy. Day after day, she continued to make my life feel more special than it ever had.

Then my business closed, and I went back to drinking. I began to feel like I was on an inexorable path to losing everything I had valued in my adult life, and even Coffee's consoling presence couldn't keep my defeatist thoughts at bay. Coffee was with me in my apartment on Saint Patrick's Day when I drank those two bottles of wine and thought I was going to die.

After a week in the hospital, I had to find some way to function normally again—if not for me, then at least for Coffee. So I began seeing a therapist. In our first session, I poured out my heart and soul and told the therapist how desperate I was to escape my feelings of inferiority. About twenty minutes into my little speech, I heard snoring. I looked over, and the therapist was fast asleep. To be fair, he looked to be about ninety years old. But still.

It was after one of my sessions with Sleeping Beauty that I realized I needed a different kind of therapy to make me feel better about myself and my life.

What I needed was another dog.

I bought another apricot poodle that I named Mickey, after one of my favorite baseball players, Mickey Mantle. At first, Coffee wasn't crazy about having a brother, but Mickey was so friendly she eventually came around. As for Mickey and me, well, we were an uncommonly good match. As extremely anxious and fearful as I was, Mickey was that calm and composed. *Nothing* bothered him. He introduced a new sense of serenity to my life. What's more, he was even more attached to me than Coffee was. Coffee would sleep in several different places in the apartment, while Mickey never budged from my bed. Wherever I went, Mickey was there with me. He became my little guy—as much a part of me as my arm or my heart.

It wasn't long after I got Mickey that I met a woman, Gladys, and fell in love. My life had crumbled around me by then, and I'd even started drinking again. But as soon as I realized Gladys and I were serious, in the summer of 2003, I quit drinking for good. We bought a house together in Westchester, and I moved in with her and her two young daughters, two dogs, and two cats. It was not, I'm afraid, a happy time for Coffee. After so many years of being my one and only companion, she now had to contend with a houseful of scampering cats and dogs. Gladys's Australian shepherd would often nip at Coffee. I was hugely protective of her, and I kept a really close eye on her, but it was obvious that she didn't love our new situation. Looking back, I think Coffee was trying her best to tell me that the situation wasn't good for *any* of us. But I didn't pay attention.

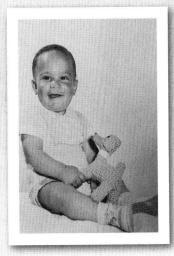

June 3, 1964, three days after my first birthday. My trademark crooked smile is already in place.

Five years old and sitting proudly with my mother, circa 1968.

Here my dad is telling my mom a funny story; nothing made me happier as a child than to sit with them.

Celebrating my Communion day with my parents in May 1971.

Here I am, in 1972, practicing my brand-new organ before bed.

I was always smiling as a kid, even at my sister Annette's wedding on March 26, 1972, when a minor argument broke out among the family. I am oblivious to all of it.

The letter I received from the thirty-third president of the United States in 1972. At nine years old, I truly believed I was on my way!

A juxtaposition of time. Here is my dad with his first new car, a 1948 Ford convertible. There I am in early 2019 with my GMC Denali, the vehicle Oliver was stolen out of.

Bartending always made me feel closer to my dad and renewed my confidence. Here are Eric and I at a private event in 2017.

Celebrating ten years with my first apricot poodle, Coffee, on September 29, 2002.

My beloved dog Louie as a puppy in 2007. He enriched my life unlike any dog before.

Mickey and Louie in 2013. Louie's sudden death at age 6 broke my heart.

After I moved into my cottage, I needed to get Mickey acclimated to Lucy's farm animals. Here he is with Anna Belle, her mini cow.

Mickey is not exactly thrilled with our new arrival, Oliver. But they soon became buddies, as Oliver was very respectful of the elder Mick.

One of our favorite trips was taking the Port Jefferson Ferry to Long Island.

CASH REWARD - $2,500

OLIVER, my beloved dog was stolen out of my car on Valentine's Day at 1119 Central Park Avenue. I ran into the cigar store to buy a few cigars. If you took him, or you know anything about his whereabouts, I beg you to please return him to me. We mean the world to each other and he must be terrified. I am offering a CASH REWARD of $2,500 no questions asked! **PLEASE, WE LOVE EACH OTHER VERY MUCH,** and go everywhere together. If you know anything about my **SWEET BABY,** please call Steve
PLEASE, I BEG YOU, DO THE RIGHT THING.

The reward poster for Oliver. Finding this picture of Oliver for my sister was one of the most painful things I had to do.

The photo that started it all—snapped by Janice Connolly on the morning of February 19, 2019. By the time we arrived, Oliver was gone.

Reunited, the single greatest moment of my life came at noon on February 21, 2019.

My sisters Laura and Nancy were there with me when Oliver jumped into my arms. Without their support—along with many others—this moment would have never happened.

A dapper Oliver is ready for his reception at Walaa's hair salon, Cleopatra, in Mount Vernon on March 2, 2019.

Here we are in Terry and Rolando's shop celebrating the return of Oliver. I am relieved, and Oliver is happy to be with me again!

One week later, on March 9, 2019, Oliver celebrates his fifth birthday with presents from his many ardent admirers.

The conversation I had with Isabela Dunlap altered my thinking on how I was going to get Oliver back. "Love will bring Oliver back to you," she said.

Manny and Walaa in Mt. Vernon with Oliver. Their kindness and compassion saved my life.

Coffee died in my arms of old age on April 29, 2007. She was fifteen, and she lived a long, happy life. I felt guilt for bringing her into such a busy, crowded house, and that guilt would stay with me forever. When my relationship began to crumble, I felt even more regret for not paying attention to what Coffee had tried to tell me. She knew me better than anyone, and she sensed I wasn't in a very good place for me. She was right—I wasn't. In fact, I was on the verge of hitting rock bottom.

After Coffee died, I found a beautiful Yorkie–shih tzu mix and brought him home with me. I named him Louie. Louie was a character with a huge personality. He was not easily trained, and he often caused trouble. He could be ferocious in the way he jumped and pranced through life, but he also had a very sweet demeanor. As a puppy he defended Mickey against the advances of the big Australian shepherd. One time the shepherd bit Louie so hard that I had to rush him to the hospital. He became a little less of a terror after that.

Something clicked with Louie and me, big-time. I almost can't explain how special our bond was. I'd felt a profoundly deep connection with all my dogs, but with Louie it almost felt like a spiritual connection. He wasn't even the type of dog I was accustomed to liking—docile, angelic, reserved. There was really no reason for me to love Louie the way I did. And yet I did—I loved him in every way possible. Louie and Mickey got me through the painful end of my relationship with Gladys and the hard times that followed.

The relationship lasted eight years. I never once drank during our time together, but even so, neither Gladys nor I were happy with each other. I probably stayed with her longer than I should have. I was forty-eight years old, which, through the dark filter of my mind, meant I was basically washed up. Who was going to be with me now? So I stayed in a relationship that often left me feeling beaten down, an echo of my difficult relationship with my father. The darkness of my past—the self-defeatism and resentment—came rushing back to the surface.

Finally, Gladys and I parted ways. I'd gone into the relationship with a fair amount of money in the bank. When I left it, I'd basically burned through it all. I needed a new place to live, so I dug through some classified ads for a rental and found my way to Lucy's cottage, with my dogs Louie and Mickey, my prized 45-rpm records, my framed letter from Harry S. Truman, and very little else.

My first night in the cottage was one of the worst nights of my life. The cottage was only three hundred square feet, and the windows were small, so it was always dark. To make matters worse, Hurricane Irene had just blown through Bedford and left me without electricity. Going from living in a big house to living in one small, pitch-black room was a shock. At the same time, it felt kind of fitting, considering the state I was in. I'd been forced to take a job as a driver, I had just a few hundred dollars in my bank account, and I had $55,000 in credit-card debt. I was no longer the executive riding in the back of a big Town Car. I was now the guy *driving* the executive to important events and meetings. I had fallen from my lofty perch, and the worst part was that it all seemed so inevitable to me. One step forward, two steps back. The Carino way.

In eight years, I took everything I had built up in my life and turned it into nothing. Absolutely nothing. Now I was stuck in a rented, one-room cottage, staring at the walls. That first day there, as I hung my framed Truman letter on the wall, I apologized to our thirty-third president. I apologized for having made him waste his time, only a short while before his death, with a nine-year-old boy's silly big dreams—dreams that never came true. That night I woke up crying more than once. Louie and Mickey looked at me with sympathetic eyes, upset, I'm sure, that even they hadn't been able to keep me from hitting rock bottom.

Not much later I came home from work one day and saw Mickey and Louie chewing on bones I'd given them earlier. I was able to get Mickey's bone away from him, but Louie growled at me when I tried to take his. So I let him keep chewing it for a while. The next day, Louie looked kind of funny to me. He was a little lethargic, and he was uncomfortable going to the bathroom. I pulled him up, held him close, and looked into his eyes. They seemed as happy and attentive as ever. I figured he had an upset stomach.

"You stay close to me tonight," I told Louie. "Tomorrow morning I'll take you to the vet. Remember, I love you very much. I love you with all my heart."

Those were the last words I ever spoke to Louie. I woke up in the morning and found him dead in the bathtub. Apparently, he had swallowed too much of the bone, and it had wrecked his intestines. In the bathroom I collapsed on the floor and buried my face in my hands. This couldn't be happening. That couldn't be Louie in the tub. But it was. On October 17, 2013, Louie was gone. The pain I felt was even more intense than the pain I endured when my mother passed away. It was one of the most devastating moments of my life.

Just four days earlier, I'd taken Mickey and Louie to the cemetery to see my mother. For some reason, Louie would not stop digging at the dirt on my mother's grave. He wasn't normally a digger, and I had no idea what he was doing. But after Louie died, I found solace in the thought that he'd been clawing at the dirt because my mother needed him with her. Louie had to leave this life in order to give his great love to someone else, on some other plane.

It also gave me peace of mind that Louie died on October 17, exactly halfway between the date my mother died (October 13) and the date my father died (October 21). I'm a big date person. Dates are important to me. So I found comfort in thinking that if Louie was taken for a reason, it was so that he could now reside safely in the arms of my parents.

The next spring, I decided to get another dog. Mickey and I were doing fine, but we both really missed Louie. "The silence is deafening," I'd tell Mickey as we rode in our suddenly quiet car together. Five days before my fifty-first birthday, after visiting my parents at the cemetery in Huntington, I went to a pet store with Gladys's daughter, whom I still visited here and there. We saw a black-and-brown Yorkie–shih tzu mix, and instantly I was smitten. He turned out to be the sweetest, most sensitive dog I'd ever known. Mickey loved him, too, even though they were eleven years apart in age. The new dog was respectful, but he also gave Mickey a new skip in his step. We were a happy team of three again.

Eventually Mickey began to slow down. I knew his time was coming. He passed away on Christmas Eve 2018, two weeks shy of his sixteenth birthday. Once again, the sense of loss was enormous and overwhelming. I thought of all of the beautiful, innocent creatures who had given me so much love and comfort, who had filled me with so much happiness and joy, who had changed my life—no, *saved* my life—every single day they were there, from my miserable teenage years to my rock-bottom days in the cottage: all of them were gone. All of them lived only in my heart now, and that was no small thing.

All of them but one.

Oliver.

Oliver was another angel who came forward and saved my life. We became inseparable, bound to each other in ways neither of us fully understood. All we knew for sure was that, as long as we were together, nothing could really hurt us. Together, we would always be okay.

And then, on Valentine's Day, Oliver was stolen.

Chapter Nineteen

Tony helped me crawl back under the fence and out of the lot. My heart was still pounding, and my body was shaking. I hadn't found Oliver, but I had the strange feeling that he was somewhere nearby. And I was afraid that if I stopped looking, even for a minute, I would lose his trail.

Or maybe I was just fooling myself.

We decided to walk around the area and see who else might know the kid in the baseball cap. We spoke with five or six people. Some of them knew the kid, some didn't, but none had any information about Oliver. Still, every single one of them was friendly and concerned. I'm not sure what I'd been expecting, but the openness of the people in the neighborhood surprised me. Their sincere interest gave me the impression that they lived under a code where if one person in the community had a problem, they *all* had a problem. It didn't even matter if you were a stranger to them; if they could help you, they would, no questions asked.

"You know something?" Tony said as we walked around the area. "The people here are genuinely concerned about you and Oliver. They're such nice people."

"I was just thinking the same thing."

Here was yet another truism that, just maybe, God was trying to open my eyes to. Yet another lesson I still needed to learn. The assumptions I'd made about the area from just driving through it were, I now realized, woefully simplistic and flat-out wrong. Yes, the person who took Oliver did something terrible. But what did I know about this person? What assumptions had I made about him? Maybe there was more to the story than I could imagine. I thought about what Isabela had told me on our drive up to Bard College—it would be love and compassion, not hate and judgment, that brought Oliver home.

My cell phone sounded. Laura was calling. She had phoned the woman who called me about Oliver—we learned her name was Janice Connolly—and arranged to go see her at the pet-grooming store where she worked. There, Janice gave her a new lead.

"Steven, go into that building and go up to apartment 3S," Laura said.

"What's in 3S?"

"It's Janice's apartment. Her husband is there now. She says he will talk to you, and she says he knows where Oliver is."

"What?"

"You have to go talk to him. And bring Tony with you."

Tony and I walked into the redbrick building through an unlocked glass front door. We walked up the stairs to the third floor. The hallway was dim and quiet. We approached 3S and stopped in front of it. I took a deep breath and knocked.

The door opened to reveal three big, burly men, all of them well over six feet tall. One of them, the one who was sitting in a chair, motioned to us. "Come on in, fellas," he said.

He introduced himself as Derek, Janice's husband.

"My wife told me you're missing a dog."

"Yes. Oliver," I said. "He was stolen."

"Okay, listen. The dog was in apartment 2W. The kid who lives there is a troublemaker. I know the dog was in that apartment because I heard him barking."

Now we knew where the kid in the baseball cap lived. The logical next step was to visit apartment 2W and look for Oliver there. But Derek told us to check the roof first.

"He might have seen the cops when they came for the car," Derek said. "Maybe he stashed the dog on the roof. Sometimes people hide stuff up there."

I thanked Derek for seeing us and for the information.

"Good luck finding your dog," he said. His two burly friends wished us good luck too.

We walked up two flights of stairs and found the door to the roof. It wasn't locked, but it was stuck, and we couldn't open it. Tony turned sideways and rammed the door with his right shoulder, like a running back plowing through a tackle. He gave the door a pretty good lick, then another. In his fur coat and dark sunglasses, he looked like an undercover cop making a drug bust. As Tony kept bashing the door, I felt a smile come over my face. I hadn't smiled in so long, it felt strange.

Tony looked at me and said, "What's so funny?"

"Look at us," I said. "This is like a movie. A guy in a fur coat trying to knock down a door. How is this my life?"

Tony smiled, too, and went back to the door. Finally he managed to push it open. We went up on the roof and looked around, the layers and layers of black tar slightly squishy beneath our feet. It didn't take long to see that Oliver wasn't there. Tony and I stood by the redbrick parapet wall and looked down over the neighborhood. The view was expansive and unobstructed; we could see for blocks and blocks in any direction. Being so high above the din of the streets felt special and peaceful. It was like, after digging down into the nitty-gritty of Oliver's theft, we were suddenly being given a broader overview. A new perspective. Both Tony and I were quiet for a while, looking out over the town.

Down on the street, five stories below, I recognized Rolando, the mechanic, looking up at me and shaking his head, as if to say, "This guy really *is* crazy."

Suddenly, it was Tony who started laughing. I laughed along with him. Neither of us felt the need to explain why we were giggling like two school kids.

"This is the first time I laughed all week," I said.

Tony looked at me and put his hand on my shoulder.

"We're gonna get him back. You know that, right?"

I didn't reply because I didn't know if I believed him.

"So what do you want to do now?" Tony asked.

"I guess we go to apartment 2W."

We walked down to the second floor, and Tony stood behind me as I got ready to knock on the door of the apartment. What if Oliver was there? What if he wasn't? I had no idea what I would do in either case. Finally I rapped the door three times with my knuckles.

After a few seconds, the door opened just a crack. I could see one eye looking at me through the small opening. Then the door opened wider, and I saw a woman in her early forties standing there.

The same woman who had helped us search for Oliver in the courtyard.

"You?" I said.

"Yeah, it's me," she said.

"But you helped me look for him," I said. "How could Oliver be here if you helped me look for him?"

"He's not here," she said. "Why would I help you look for him if I already had him?"

"But someone told me they heard my dog in here."

"There's no dog here."

I was confused. Derek had been certain he heard a dog in 2W. And he knew for a fact the kid in the baseball cap lived there.

"Well, maybe it's your son who has him?" I asked.

The woman's demeanor quickly changed.

"Everyone in this building blames my son for everything, and I'm sick and tired of it," she said. "You don't know this area. You don't live here. You don't know my son. So, no, I don't have your dog."

With that, she closed the door.

My first thought was that Oliver wasn't in her apartment. If he'd been there, he would have heard my voice and barked. He would have let me know he was there. Unless, of course, he was somehow subdued, or maybe even drugged. The only way I could know for sure was to look through the apartment myself. But I didn't want to knock on the door again and get in a screaming match. Instead, Tony and I went down to the street to figure out our next move.

Laura and Lucy were outside the building; they had just returned from White Plains with more flyers. I filled them in on what had happened. Laura believed the first thing we should do was fan out and put up flyers. Every window, every pole, every corner. That way, we could spread the word about the $5,000 reward and give people more incentive to come forward. We each took a small stack of flyers and began taping them up.

After I put up a single flyer, though, I had to stop. I hadn't had flyer duty yet, so I'd never had to look too hard at the flyer itself. When I finally did, the big, bright picture of Oliver was too much for me to bear. It had been days since I'd had a close look at Oliver's innocent face, and suddenly seeing him on the flyer hit me harder than I expected. I felt my knees weaken again, followed by a sudden surge of anger.

"I can't do this," I told Tony. "I have to go back to 2W."

Then I was in the redbrick building again, marching up to the second floor. I was by myself this time; I felt it should be just me, talking to the woman one-on-one. I knocked on the door and heard the shuffling of feet. When the door opened, this time a man was standing there. The woman was standing behind him.

"Look," I said, "all I want is my dog. I need my dog. Where is my dog?"

"We don't have your dog," the man said calmly.

"A guy in the building told me he was here. Maybe he's not here now, but he was here, that I know. All I want is to get him back and take him home. That's all. I don't care about anything else. I just need my dog."

The woman stepped forward and opened the door wider. "You can come in and look for him if you like," she said. "But we don't have him."

"There's a five-thousand-dollar reward," I said. "I will give you the money right now. Just, please, please, tell me where he is."

I was starting to get emotional, and the man and woman looked at me with unmistakable sympathy. They weren't mean or angry. Heck, they didn't even have to open the door for me, much less invite me into their home. Yet they patiently listened to me and seemed genuinely sorry for me. Standing there, I realized I believed them. I didn't have to search their apartment; Oliver wasn't there. And, obviously, if their son was the person who took Oliver, they would be protective of him. I understood that too. My hope was that they would at least have an idea where Oliver might be, but they remained adamant that they didn't.

"We know how much you love that dog," the man said. "We just don't know where he is."

By then, Laura had come in and joined me in the hallway. I thanked the couple in 2W and asked them to let me know if they heard anything about Oliver. They promised they would and closed the door. Laura and I walked downstairs and out on the street.

"So what do you want to do now?" Laura asked.

"I don't know," I said. "All I know is I don't want to leave the area yet."

The four of us got into Tony's Range Rover and talked strategy. It was late afternoon by then, and soon it would be dark. I spotted the two police officers who had impounded the stolen SUV walking toward us down the block. When they saw us in Tony's car, they came over. A police captain was with them. I filled him in on our eventful day, right up to my last visit to apartment 2W. The police captain listened and nodded his head. I got the feeling he couldn't quite believe anyone would go to this much trouble for a stolen dog. Or maybe he looked at the four of us, including Tony in his big fur coat, and thought we were, I don't know, a little eccentric. Then the captain noticed one of our flyers taped to a telephone pole.

"Is that your dog?" he asked.

"Yes, that's Oliver," I said.

"Five thousand dollars?" the captain asked, shaking his head. "I wouldn't offer that much if it were my wife."

I wasn't in the mood for jokes, but still, I got a chuckle out of that.

"Okay, tell you what," the captain said. "We'll go up and check out the apartment. You guys stay down here."

Thirty minutes later, the policemen were back. They said they'd searched under beds, in closets, everywhere in apartment 2W, and Oliver wasn't there. I wasn't surprised; I already knew he wasn't.

"So what are your plans now?" the captain asked.

"We're going to stick around here a while longer," I said.

The captain smiled and shook his head again. I think he continued to be amused by us. The indefatigable stolen-dog hunters. He warned us to be careful and left us to our vigil. Now it was dark and getting colder. We stayed in Tony's car and just talked.

A few minutes later, a car pulled up alongside us. It was Alan, come to pick up Lucy and drive her home. I hugged her and thanked her for her help. I told her how much it meant to me that she had spent the day with me searching for Oliver.

"We will find him, Steven," Lucy assured me.

After Lucy and Alan left, Laura, Tony, and I sat in the warm Range Rover and reflected on our surreal day. We talked about how friendly and accommodating everyone was, even the couple in apartment 2W. Tony and I told Laura the story of our adventure on the roof. The day had been so filled with twists and turns that I never stopped to think that I hadn't eaten a thing. We'd all been on the go since Janice Connolly's phone call. Taking a break hadn't occurred to us.

Just then a car pulled up alongside us. It was Alan again. I wondered why he'd come back, and I hoped nothing was wrong. Lucy got out of the car holding a big, flat white box.

"We brought pizza!" she said cheerily.

Lucy hadn't just brought pizza. She'd brought a cheese pie from the legendary family-owned Johnny's Pizzeria on Mount Vernon's West Lincoln Avenue. I'd heard about the place, and it was famous for its appetizing pizza. It had been in Mount Vernon for more than seventy-five years, and it only sold pizza by the pie, not the slice. When the sweet smell of cheese and sauce filled the Range Rover, I felt something that resembled genuine excitement. We each took a slice and bit into what was, for me, the single most delicious thing I'd ever tasted—ever. I don't know if it was the circumstances or the pizza, but to this day that slice remains my most memorable meal.

I looked around at Lucy and Alan and Laura and Tony and told myself to take note of the moment. *These people, these wonderful people—they are here for you, Steven, I thought. Think of their thoughtfulness, one human to another—what a beautiful thing that is. Aren't you just blown away by them? By all of them? By the mechanics and the little kids who went around yelling Oliver's name, and by Janice and Derek and all the people on the street who stopped to talk to you? By your sister Laura and your pal Tony? By Alan and Lucy bringing pizza? How could you ever think you were all alone, Steven? Can't you tell you're not alone?*

Before we decided to call it a day, I spotted Rolando and Terry outside their store and went over to talk to them.

"Guys, I didn't find Oliver," I told them. "But you know what? I am so touched by how everyone helped me. The people here are amazing."

"Well, you're not accusing anyone," Rolando said. "You're not screaming at anyone. You're being nice. It works both ways."

"Rolando, let me ask you this: Do you think Oliver is alive? Do you think he's still alive?"

Rolando put his arm around me, as if we'd known each other for years.

"Let me tell you how the hood works," he said. "Someone has your dog. They're trying to figure out how to get your dog back to you without getting pinched for the stolen car. They also know the dog is worth five thousand dollars. They ain't gonna kill the dog. They just have to figure out a way to make this work. But believe me—that dog ain't dead. That's not how it works out here."

Rolando was giving me something that had been almost impossible for me to find: hope.

It pained me to finally have to leave Mount Vernon and drive back to Laura's house without Oliver. I tried not to think of where he might be or what had happened to him after he was spotted in the SUV. Had the kid in the baseball cap seen the police officers towing the stolen SUV and gotten scared? Had he stashed Oliver in the courtyard in case the cops came looking for him? And had Oliver made his way through the broken fence and just run off? Or had the kid already sold Oliver to God knew who? I forced myself to stop going over the possibilities. There was no point to it. I just had to hold on to the slight bit of hope I had, and keep searching.

Back at Laura's, I learned that my post on Facebook from earlier that day, the one titled "I Am Caught in a Storm," had received dozens and dozens of comments. Some people said the post made them cry. Others who also read an update about our day that Nancy posted said they were going to go to Mount Vernon with $250 of their own money to try to buy Oliver. Some asked if they could share my post with their prayer groups. Nearly everyone offered their love and prayers and thanked me for baring my soul.

Plus, we were over ten thousand shares and likes.

Something was happening. Something bigger than me. My eyes

were being opened to a greater truth about the world, an insight into our shared humanity, a closeup look at the extraordinary power of love and empathy. All of which allowed me to conclude that though I still hadn't found my beloved Oliver, that day in Mount Vernon, New York, was unquestionably one of the most beautiful days of my life.

The Search: Day Six
February 20

Oliver isn't crazy about baths. He doesn't hate them, but he's clearly not a fan. He gets quiet when I bring him into the bathroom and lower him into the tub. I test the water to make sure it's perfectly warm, and then I slide Oliver beneath the faucet, and when I look at his face, his sad-eyed expression says, Do we really have to do this? I mean, I don't smell all that bad.

And yet he doesn't struggle or squirm or try to get out of it. He just endures it. That's because Oliver has a certain resolve to him. He knows it's going to happen, so he just gets through it. I've always thought Oliver picked up that trait from me. I've learned how to grit my teeth and get through tough situations, and I take pride in that resolve. I get beat up, but I come right back. I might get down on myself, but I keep going. I think my strength and resolve fed into Oliver and helped make him the tough little critter he is.

Of course, it works both ways. Oliver's resolve feeds me too. His strength makes me strong. I think we both know that when bad things happen, we will be able to get through it—together. And knowing that makes it easier for us to keep going, to endure, to believe.

Chapter Twenty

The day after Oliver disappeared, I took everything that reminded me of him and put it away in a closet. I took his toys and his towel out of the SUV, his red doggie bowl and his little mat with a map on it, his blue dog blanket, his dog bones, and his rubber fire-hydrant chew toy. I put them all where I wouldn't have to see them. But even the SUV itself reminded me of Oliver, so I decided to use it only for driving jobs and take my old, gold Mercury Grand Marquis everywhere else. I told myself all of this was only temporary, that when Oliver came back, I'd bring out all his things and buy him a ton of new stuff too. But, as the days rolled by, I couldn't stop myself from imagining the day when I'd have to throw Oliver's things away.

When I woke up Wednesday morning in Laura's house, I didn't feel any more certain about my chances of getting Oliver back. But I *did* feel better about the way I was handling his loss. Slowly, I'd seen my anger and bitterness give way to more positive feelings. With each new act of kindness directed at Oliver and me, a little more of the darkness in my soul receded. The way I would put it is to say that I woke on Wednesday with a lot of love in my heart. Love and forgiveness. This felt like someone lifting a ten-ton weight off my chest. I was able to think more clearly and strip away the negativity that made it so hard for me to see straight in the days following Oliver's disappearance.

Most importantly, after a few days of either berating him or righteously ignoring him, I felt like I was finally able to talk to God again and ask for his help.

"God, I'm sorry for the words I spoke," I said aloud, looking skyward. "I'm sorry I doubted you. I need to come back to you now. I know you were watching over me all along."

I said something similar to the loved ones I'd lost.

"Mom, Dad, Frank, I'm sorry for the way I acted. I still don't fully understand why, but I woke up today without any hatred in my heart. I'm sorry, and I need your help."

Then I told Laura what I had planned for the day.

"I need to go back to Mount Vernon," I said. "But I need to go there alone. Just me. Someone knows more than they are telling us. I need to go there by myself and find out."

My first few months living in Lucy's small cottage were, as I mentioned, difficult. It took me a long time to stop dwelling on how far I'd fallen, how much I'd lost, and how alone I felt. I was so depressed and morose that I was blind to the natural charms and beauty of Lucy's five-acre spread.

For instance, Lucy had a collection of ten or so goats and sheep who were basically invisible to me early on but who eventually began to feel like my friends. I'd see them every day coming out of their barn, ready to graze, and I'd walk over and say hello. I became able to tell them apart, and I realized that I was always happy to see them. They were funny and never seemed too upset about anything, and that cheered me up. They made me take myself less seriously.

Before long, I was feeding them slices of white bread, summoning them with my best rendition of a goat call. They grew to trust me and started rushing over and surrounding me when they heard the call. I fed them by hand, glad to have such a moment of intimacy and connection. They forced me to appreciate the beauty surrounding us—a lovely flat pasture full of wildflowers, old trees, cats and rabbits scooting about, gentle breezes, quiet afternoons: a little slice of paradise. It took a long time, but I finally opened my eyes to what I *had* instead of dwelling on what I'd lost.

And when I did, I realized my life wasn't over.

That is about the time I began rereading a particular passage of the Bible that I remembered from many years before: Proverbs 3. Verse 3 had stayed with me over the years. "Let love and faithfulness never leave you; bind them around your neck, write them on the tablet of your heart." That was one of the most beautiful lines I'd ever read. It felt like a good time for me to revisit it, so I picked up a Bible and looked it over a few times.

I decided I wanted to try to memorize all thirty-five verses of Proverbs 3. I'd always prided myself on my memorization skills, starting, of course, with the US presidents. But I hadn't tried to memorize anything for more than forty years—since my mother died. Now, here was something else besides the presidents that mattered to me. Why not commit it to memory? If nothing else, it would be a way to keep my mind sharp.

At the time, I still had two dogs, Mickey and Oliver. I would take them outside and recite Proverbs 3 to them as we walked. I'd explain some of the lines to them, or at least the way I interpreted them. I would tell them why a certain passage spoke so strongly to me. During these walks with Mickey and Oliver, I realized that I felt something like contentment. That's when I figured out I wasn't at rock bottom anymore. I still had a long way to go to have the kind of life I thought I wanted, but at least I wasn't flat on my back. I had Mickey and Oliver, and I had the goats and sheep, and I had Proverbs 3. And those were pretty wonderful things to have.

My routine with Mickey and Oliver was interrupted when Mickey entered his final days. He had begun to slow down, and I knew I was coming up on the time when I'd have to make that dreaded decision—the time when I would have to let Mickey go. My only hope was that it would be obvious to me when that time came.

And it was. I woke up early on the morning of Christmas Eve 2018, and I looked at Mickey, and I knew in my heart this would be our last day together. I put on one of my favorite songs, Buddy Holly's "True Love Ways," and I held Mickey to my chest and danced with him to the music. Then I sat with him on my bed so we could have our last meaningful talk.

"Mickey, you have to go away now, but you have to know that I am never, ever going to forget you, okay?" I said, trying not to cry too hard and upset Mickey. "I want to give you something now, and I want you to take it with you. And I want you to know that as long as you have it with you, you will always be with me. We will always be together."

And then I leaned in close to Mickey and softly recited Proverbs 3:5–6 to him from memory:

> Trust in the LORD with all your heart
>   and lean not on your own understanding;
> in all your ways submit to him,
>   and he will make your paths straight.

When I was done with all thirty-five verses, it occurred to me that this was the very reason I had memorized Proverbs 3—so that I'd be ready to give these words to Mickey when the time came.

As we headed into the new year, Oliver and I were left to mourn Mickey and give each other solace and comfort. I continued reciting Proverbs 3 to Oliver during our walks, and I continued to feel a real sense of contentment as we hiked down leafy, peaceful East Field Drive, joined occasionally by the handsome white horse owned by a neighbor. Sometimes a soft winter snow sprinkled our walks.

Our friendship blossomed during our walk and talks, and Oliver became a part of me, necessary for my well-being, central to my existence. This was the first time in a while that I'd had only one dog, and something about the exclusivity of our one-to-one relationship strengthened our bond. Aside from work, I rarely went anywhere without Oliver. We were, without exaggeration, best friends. I lived in a town filled with sprawling estates and huge mansions, yet with Oliver, I truly felt like the wealthiest man in the world. I'd even tell him this on our walks: "Oliver, I swear to you, even though we live in a tiny cottage, we are the wealthiest fellas in Bedford!" And Oliver would look up at me and wag his tail, as if to say, *Stee, I agree.*

One passage, from Proverbs 3:11–12, seemed perfectly appropriate to my situation at that time. It was the part about discipline: "My son, do not despise the Lord's discipline, and do not resent his rebuke, because the Lord disciplines those he loves, as a father the son he delights in."

I'd spent a lot of time thinking about this passage, and I found it incredibly comforting: the idea that life's hardest challenges are, in a way, gifts from the Lord—evidence of his great love for us. I thought back on all the ways I'd been tested in my life—my mother's death, my father's rages, my problems with drinking—and I recast all those times as evidence of God's divine love. The message I took from these words was profound: to be human is to endure hardship, and to endure hardship means that we are alive. And being alive is the greatest gift. God's challenges, in the end, are really blessings. They are how we learn what it means to be one of God's children.

Thinking of my life through this lens, and understanding that I had made it through all the hardships without losing my faith in God, also made me think that perhaps the worst tests of my life were already behind me.

"You know what, Oliver?" I said aloud during one of our walks. "I think the hard part is over for us. I'm not saying I won't be tested again, but the real hard stuff . . . I think maybe I'm over the hump with that kind of challenge. I've been through a lot, you know? So maybe I'm over all that."

Oliver changed my way of looking at my life. My cottage was no longer a tiny refuge for a loser; it was a magical place to live. My job as a driver was no longer a job for a washed-up has-been; it was dignified work bringing people safely to and from their destinations. I no longer knew no one in town; I had friends and people who liked me.

Proverbs 3 mentions that wisdom and understanding are the most valuable assets we have in life. Somehow, thanks to Oliver, I was beginning to see that this is true. It isn't so much what you *have* but what you *believe* that defines who you are and how you live. With Oliver, I believed, perhaps for the first time ever, that I was wealthy, respectable, and content.

Just a short time later, Oliver was stolen.

I was being tested again. And on that awful night in the parking lot outside the cigar store, I recited perhaps the most powerful lines of Proverbs 3:25–26: "Have no fear of sudden disaster or of the ruin that overtakes the wicked, for the LORD will be at your side and will keep your foot from being snared." I thought of those words and I wondered if, given what had just happened, I truly believed them. Keep my foot from being snared? Really? Was I kidding myself? The Lord at my side? Well, where was he when Oliver was taken?

Had I just memorized a bunch of words that really meant nothing?

The "sudden disaster" of Oliver's disappearance took everything I thought I'd learned about life and God and mixed it all up into a cloud of confusion. I no longer knew what I believed in or what I held dear. If I could lose Oliver in the blink of an eye, then there was no such thing in life as stability. No such thing as contentment.

No such thing as faith.

An Elvis Presley song, written by Marty Robbins, came to mind— "You Gave Me a Mountain." The lyrics go like this: "It's been one hill after another . . . . But this time, Lord, you gave me a mountain."

By taking away Oliver, the Lord had given me a mountain. And I just didn't know if I could climb it.

I got into my old Mercury and set out for Mount Vernon by myself. But this time, I brought something with me. I brought Proverbs 3. I'd memorized it, and now it was time to put it into practice. I was determined to demonstrate the proverb through my actions.

On the way, I went over my plan. More than anything, I wanted to talk to the person who actually took Oliver: the kid in the baseball cap. My hope was to somehow find him and let him know exactly what he had done to me, the damage he had wrought—but not in an accusatory way. Whatever I did, whoever I confronted, I wanted to be able to do it with love and forgiveness in my heart. But how to square the circle? How could I share the enormous pain Oliver's theft had caused without being judgmental or accusing? How could I push for more information about Oliver without conveying anger and frustration? I didn't have the answer, so I prayed to God.

"God, give me the strength I need to be truthful but not spiteful. Help me to use *your* tools, God, to find Oliver."

I parked in front of the redbrick building on Norton Street. Outside it was cloudy and snowy and cold. I went into the building and up to the second floor. As I'd done the day before, I paused outside the door of 2W to catch my breath and steady myself. I had no idea what to expect or how I'd be received. After all, the woman in 2W must have known I was the one who sent police officers up to her apartment. Would she slam the door in my face? Would I blame her if she did? After one last deep breath, I knocked.

The door opened, and she was there. I didn't even know her name. She seemed almost amused to see me.

"Oh, it's you," she said.

"Do you mind if I talk to you for a minute?" I said. "Just me and you."

She looked at me and smiled.

"Not at all," she said. "Come in."

Chapter Twenty-One

Her name, I learned, was Donna. She looked to be around forty years old, and she was soft-spoken, with a kind, round face. Her apartment opened into a living room, beyond which were the bedrooms. To the left was the kitchen. The place was cluttered with clothes and sneakers and toys. Donna's two young children, who had helped me look for Oliver the day before, were running around the living room, playing. Before Donna could invite me in farther, I stood in the entrance hall and started talking.

"Look, I just want to say that whoever took Oliver, I don't think they did it out of evil or hatred," I said. "I think they just didn't understand my bond with Oliver. When he was taken, I was destroyed. I mean, *destroyed*. He took my heart. He took my *life*. The person who took Oliver *took my life*. And I think you understand that because you were out there yesterday helping me find him. Now I know Oliver isn't here. And I am not saying your son took him. But you need to know that I am not leaving this street until I find my dog. And I need to know if your son knows anything. So please, Donna, please—may I talk to your son?"

The emotions poured out. I was crying again. Even Donna wiped away a tear. She looked at me without a trace of anger or annoyance and called over her youngest child.

"Go get Del," she told her.

The girl ran to the rear of the apartment and soon came back out. A young man walked behind her. He was tall and thin, and he looked about seventeen, though he might have been older. He had a handsome face, and he was wearing a baseball cap. He leaned against a wall in the living room and looked at me with no expression.

"This is Del," Donna said.

"Hi, Del. I'm Steven," I said.

Del nodded but said nothing.

"I know they have been telling you my son did this, but they blame him for everything," Donna said.

"I understand," I said, looking at Del. "I'm not saying you took Oliver. I don't care if you did. All I care is that I get Oliver back. You gotta understand . . . you have to understand . . ."

I grasped for the right words as my heart broke open.

"Del, listen to me. I'm not married. I have no family of my own. I drive people to airports for a living. And I live with my dog. That's it. That's all I have. That's my life. So whoever took Oliver, they didn't just take my cell phone or car or computer. They took my whole life. You're looking at a broken man. And that's why I'm here. I have love in my heart, and I need your help. Del, I'm asking you to help me find Oliver. Can you help me, please?"

Del looked down at his feet. It appeared to me like he was wiping away a tear.

"Yes, I'll help," he said. "I'll make a couple of calls."

I was overcome by a feeling of gratitude. Gratitude for Donna, for her son Del, and for her whole family. Gratitude and affection and, above all, connection. Regardless of what came of this meeting, I realized that the people in apartment 2W were not outsiders or strangers or enemies, as I'd once pegged them to be. They were simply people with their own problems, some much worse than mine, struggling to make lives for themselves in challenging conditions, trying, like everyone else, to find a path through the darkness. Donna was simply a mother trying to raise a family, and it wasn't always easy. It was often very hard, and yet she pushed on. And she did what she could to keep her family together.

Yet, despite their own hardships, they welcomed me into their home and listened to my story and offered to help me find Oliver. Even if it was Del who took Oliver—and I believed it was—they didn't have to let me into their apartment or help me look for my dog. They could have shut me out and refused to talk to me. They could have treated me as the outsider, the stranger, the enemy. But they didn't. They welcomed me, and they empathized with me, and they even cried with me. And they offered me their help.

Did they do all this out of fear that Del would be arrested for stealing the dog and the SUV? Did they do it because they knew where Oliver was and wanted the $5,000 reward?

Possibly.

But I chose to see it otherwise. I chose to believe those tears were real. I chose to believe that when Del took Oliver, he didn't expect to fall in love with him, but he did anyway because Oliver was the kind of dog who burrows his way into your heart. So when I told Del what losing Oliver did to me, I believed he understood what I was saying and even regretted what he'd done, and *that's* why he agreed to help me.

Could I have been wrong? I guess so. But I don't think I was.

I took out my wallet, pulled out $200, and handed it to Donna. She was surprised and could barely bring herself to take it.

"What's this for?" she asked.

"It's for you. For helping me. And for your kids. Buy them something. I want you to have it."

Donna took the money and wiped away tears again.

When I finally left apartment 2W and walked down the front stoop out into the cold air, I felt gratitude for Donna and her family, but also something else. I felt—and this may sound strange—like my entire life had been preparing me and leading me to this very moment, on 328 Norton Street, in apartment 2W, with this family.

Suddenly, everything that had been confusing seemed clear. Why? Because in that moment, God allowed me to use *his* tools— love, kindness, compassion—to accomplish what I set out to do. He put me to a test, and I got through it without judgment or resentment. God let me use all the pain and anguish of my life to make an honest connection with someone who, only six days earlier, I had raged against. This, I realized, was a gift. A gift bestowed not on the kid in the baseball cap but on *me*.

What was that gift?

I believed it was the gift of *wisdom*.

I thought of another passage from Proverbs 3:

> Blessed are those who find wisdom,
>> those who gain understanding,
> for she is more profitable than silver
>> and yields better returns than gold.
> She is more precious than rubies;
>> nothing you desire can compare with her. (vv. 13–15)

Imagine that—wisdom is more valuable than silver or gold. Nothing we desire can compare to wisdom. But why? Why is wisdom so valuable? What does wisdom give us?

I thought back on all the trials of my life. I pictured my mother sitting in her recliner in the den, riddled with cancer, torn by her pain. I thought of my father in his rages, screaming at me, his face twisted by something he couldn't understand. I thought of my younger self, stuck in a room somewhere, too self-doubting to venture out into the world. I saw an image of me in a hospital bed, with tubes sticking out of my body, pulling out the poisons I had put there myself. And all of it—all the pain and anguish—made sense to me now. For it all led me to this moment, when I found the wisdom to see these trials for what they were—opportunities to show my trust and faith in God.

If you can endure tribulations and, as it says in Proverbs 3:3, "let love and faithfulness never leave you," you will gain the wisdom that brings true well-being.

If you can "bind them around your neck" and "write them on the tablet of your heart," you will never again feel lost or alone.

The events of my life, and the words of Proverbs 3, all came together that morning in Mount Vernon, and they allowed me to form a thought that had been absolutely unthinkable when the week began.

I understand now why Oliver had to be taken.

I walked to the deli on the corner to get a cup of coffee. Then I called my sister Laura.

"They want to help us," I said. "They're going to help us."

Laura said she was coming down to join me. In about half an hour she pulled up and parked in front of the redbrick building. She stepped out of her car and gave me a hug.

"I'd like to talk to Donna too," she said.

I understood how invested Laura was in finding Oliver. She could read me better than anyone, and she knew how much of a wreck I was. She knew what my life would be like if I didn't get Oliver back. Now she wanted the chance to plead my case directly to Donna. Laura wanted to do anything and everything she possibly could to bring Oliver home.

So we went back to apartment 2W. Donna graciously welcomed us in, and she and Laura spoke in the kitchen.

"My brother is twelve years younger than me," Laura said. "Our mother died when he was young, and I'm very protective of him. And I just want you to know that if we don't get his dog back, my brother will never be the same. That's why I'm asking you for help. I need you to help my brother."

Donna looked down and was quiet for a moment.

"I was brought up in foster homes," she finally said in a soft voice. "I went from one to the next to the next. I didn't have a family of my own. Now I do. And I know that sometimes my son makes mistakes, but he is a good person. He is a *good* person. And we are all trying to do the best we can."

It was like we had come to an understanding. We were from very different worlds, and sad circumstances had brought us together, but now we all wanted the same thing.

We all just wanted our families to be intact.

Donna and Laura spoke some more. When it was time to go, they hugged each other, and they both wiped away tears.

"What are you going to do now?" Donna asked.

"We're going to wait outside in the car," I said. "We'll be there all day."

"Steven, Laura, I know my home is a mess," Donna said.

"Your home is not a mess," Laura said.

"It's not a fancy home. But it's cold outside, and if it gets too cold for you, please come back. I will make you hot chocolate."

Back on the street, I told Laura I believed Del was going to call whoever he'd stashed Oliver with, get Oliver back, and arrange a meeting with us to hand him over. I truly believed that's what would happen. I couldn't be certain Del knew where Oliver was—he could have dumped him somewhere when the cops showed up—but I had to believe he had some idea how to get Oliver back, and that he was going to do what he could to return Oliver to us.

"All we can do is wait," I said.

Laura brought a bundle of flyers, and we walked around putting them up. Rolando, the mechanic, came out of his shop and waved when he saw us.

"You won't leave, will you?" he said with a smile.

"Not without Oliver," I said.

A little later we ran into the two beat cops who impounded the SUV. When they saw us, they smiled too.

"You guys again?" one of them said.

"We're not leaving," I said.

It was getting cold out, so when we finished putting up flyers we sat in Laura's car. Laura kept some flyers and handed them to people who walked by. Otherwise, there wasn't much we could do but wait. Wait for Del or someone to contact us about Oliver. Now and then,

I'd get out of the car and walk around and look for Oliver, mostly just to stretch my legs. But for most of that day, Laura and I sat in her car and waited for something to happen.

A couple of hours in, I got a text alert on my phone. It was from Helen, the girl who was upset that Oliver got stolen and had sent me a picture of her white Labrador to cheer me up.

"Did you find Oliver yet?" she asked in her text.

"Not yet. Keep your fingers crossed."

"I will. Hang in there. You'll get him back."

The hours passed. Three o'clock. Four o'clock. Before I knew it, it was dark outside, and still no sign of Del or anyone who might have Oliver. The longer we waited, the harder it became for me to fight off the bad thoughts. One scenario, in particular, haunted me.

Earlier in the week, Janice Connolly had told Laura that the kid in the baseball cap often hung out with some kids from Brooklyn. It was possible, Janice said, that he had given them Oliver to hide, and now Oliver was in Brooklyn somewhere. I couldn't bear the thought of Oliver being held captive in the sprawling borough of Brooklyn. If he was there, I feared, we would never find him. My gut was telling me Oliver was still nearby—or was that just wishful thinking? I pushed the idea of Brooklyn out of my brain as forcefully as I could and tried to focus on what Del had told me: "I'll make a couple of calls." That meant Del knew something about Oliver's whereabouts. He *had* to know something, didn't he? I had to trust that Del would be true to his word and bring Oliver back to me. I had to keep the faith.

But, boy, was it hard.

So we waited. It was seven o'clock now, which meant I'd spent about ten hours in Mount Vernon, on Norton Street, just waiting. I searched the face of every person who walked down the block— man, woman, young, old—hoping to see some sign of complicity in Oliver's theft. But there was nothing in their faces but indifference to my plight. Meanwhile, the increasing cold and darkening night reflected nature's indifference. Time itself was indifferent. The world spun on, oblivious to my little drama playing out on Norton Street.

And then, around eight o'clock, a white car drove slowly past us and stopped a car length in front. Laura and I watched with breaths held as the red brake lights came on.

Then, ever so slowly, the car began to back up.

Time stopped. Everything happened slowly. The car kept rolling backward until it was parallel to us. The windows were tinted, and it was too dark to see through them. *Is this it?* I thought. *Is Oliver in that car?*

Finally, the car stopped, and the driver's-side window came down. The driver was a young woman.

"Are you Oliver's father?" she asked.

Just then, a dog jumped onto the passenger seat and stuck his head out the window.

A small brown-and-black dog.

A dog that looked exactly like . . .

"Oliver!" I shouted.

I flung open my door and jumped out, hitting my head pretty hard on the doorframe. The quick movement startled the dog in the window, and he scampered out of view.

"Oliver?" I said. "Oliver, it's me!"

"Oh no," the woman said. "This isn't Oliver. This is my little boy, Rocky."

Rocky? I thought. *Who's Rocky? What's going on? This dog looks exactly like Oliver!*

"I've been following your story on Facebook since Oliver got stolen," the woman explained. "I drove around all day looking for him. I'm so sorry for confusing you with Rocky."

I looked hard at her dog. It wasn't Oliver. I could tell that now. He was sitting on his mother's lap, and he didn't want anything to do with me. I got back in Laura's car, my body trembling, my chest heavy and tight. The shock of seeing this other nearly identical Yorkie–shih tzu, and believing for a moment that it was Oliver—it was devastating. *Devastating.* I looked at Laura, and I could tell she was feeling the same way. I saw the bewilderment in her eyes, and I knew what she was thinking. To be this close, *this close*, and have it be just another miss—it seemed like an impossibly cruel joke.

The woman apologized two or three more times, and I could tell she felt sincerely bad. She explained that she'd followed our story and decided to drive around Mount Vernon on a snowy night, Rocky in tow, hoping to spot Oliver. What kindness from a stranger! I guess she just didn't anticipate our reaction to seeing Rocky. Certainly, she couldn't have known how defeating this moment of false hope would be for us.

We thanked her for doing so much to help us, and after she left, we sat in Laura's car in silence. It was late, and it was cold, and it was suddenly obvious to both of us that no one was coming any time soon to hand over Oliver. What began as a promising day, almost a *transcendent* day, would end as just another sad X mark on the calendar.

Six full days, and no Oliver.

"Let's go home," Laura said.

On the way, I was powerless to hold off the dark thoughts. I had truly believed this was the day I would get Oliver back. I'd used God's tools, I'd emptied my heart of hate, I'd done the right thing—yet the result was the same: no Oliver. As if to drive home the point, we'd even been given an Oliver look-alike, only so our momentary joy could be snatched away. Why? What lesson, exactly, was God trying to teach me with *that* stunt? And what about Proverbs 3? Had I really found some kind of wisdom, or had I just deluded myself into thinking I had? The clarity of earlier that day disappeared, replaced by more confusion. Confusion and hopelessness.

A new thought formed. *You know you're not getting Oliver back, Steven, don't you? Surely you must know that by now.*

Chapter Twenty-Two

He would have thought, as he was taken out of my car and put in the white SUV, *Oh no. This isn't good. This isn't good at all. Because the person who has me, the person who is taking me away, is not Stee.*

He would have thought, as he found himself in a strange apartment in a strange building, with two young kids petting him and fawning over him and a mother arguing with her son, *I'll do what I'm told. I'll sit where they put me. I won't make noise. If they want to pet me, I'll let them pet me. And in time, Stee will come and get me. Then we'll go back to how it was.*

He would have spent parts of five days in that apartment, with children who grew to love him and a woman who fed him and gave him water and saw to it that he wasn't harmed. The rest of the time, he would have been in the white SUV with the person who had taken him, the kid in the baseball cap, as the kid drove around and tried to sell him for $250. He wouldn't have understood what was happening or why he was there, but he would have continued to play it cool, to go with the flow. *Just bide your time. Don't bark or whimper. Stee is on the way.*

Certainly, he wouldn't have known the motives of the person who took him. He wouldn't have known why he was taken to the apartment. He wouldn't have understood the arguments that followed, the notion that a stolen dog couldn't remain in the apartment. It would have meant nothing to him when someone said, "You have to get rid of that dog."

But I believe he *would* have understood that the people who had him were not evil, and even that the kid who took him was growing fond of him. He would have noticed the care the kid took to put him in the SUV and take him back out. The presence of kindness is never lost on a dog, and every caring gesture is accepted as proof of the ancient bond between man and dog—the idea that dogs are "man's best friend." Surely, he would have kept up his guard and not forgotten that he was far from home. But I believe he would have understood that, given the circumstances, he was relatively safe.

But then, on the fifth day, there would have been the commotion. The woman and the son standing beside the apartment's front windows, with their clear view of the street in front, watching as two police officers traced the plates on the stolen white Subaru. Hiding under the sofa, perhaps, Oliver would have sensed the panic, the urgency. He would have heard the hushed, angry words. And as two arms reached out to pick him up and hustle him to the back of the apartment, he would have felt afraid, truly afraid, perhaps even more afraid than when he was taken from the SUV.

This can't be good. Where is he taking me? Where is Stee?

And then—when he was perhaps held tightly with just one arm, while the kid in the baseball cap climbed through a back window and eased down the fire escape ladder, jumping the last few feet to the ground of the courtyard—he would have been wide-eyed with fear. Everything would have been moving too fast for him. Then he would have been left there, on a small patch of grass surrounded by dirt and trash and debris, in a tiny fenced-in courtyard in the back of the building, as the kid in the cap ran off somewhere to flee the cops looking for him.

He would have sat there for a while, terrified, taking it in. The new smells—old garbage, old food, empty beer cans. The new noises— car horns, a radio playing in the shop across the lot. After a while he would have stood up and gingerly walked around, sniffing things, getting his bearings, his tail tucked down, his ears pinned back. He would have peered around constantly for threats and stayed ready to run. He would have waited and listened, for what, he couldn't know.

And then, as more time passed with no activity around him, he would have expanded his circle, venturing a little farther from the spot where he was dropped, sniffing more things, trying to get a fix on his surroundings. He would have stepped carefully around the cans and bottles and avoided the slabs of rubber and wood. And when he came to the mangled chain-link fence that separated the courtyard from the vacant lot next to the redbrick building, he would have approached it with utmost caution, letting his nose do the work from afar, before getting any closer.

He would have seen the rip at the bottom of the fence that left just enough room for him to squeeze through.

And he would have thought, *Well, if Stee's not coming, then I guess I will go find Stee.*

Later that day, when the cops had gone and the mother and her young children came looking for him and calling out his name, they would have found only an empty courtyard. And the following day, when the kid in the baseball cap began in earnest to try to find Oliver again, it really wouldn't have mattered. Because by the time they all started looking for him, Oliver was already long gone.

Chapter Twenty-Three

They were born nine thousand miles from Mount Vernon, in countries across the Red Sea from each other.

Manny was raised in Jordan, where his father owned a clothing factory. He was sixteen and knew just a little bit of English when his mother brought him to the United States to live with his aunt in Yonkers. Three of his siblings were already in the United States because their parents believed they would have more opportunities there. Manny soon understood why. Even in high school, he came to believe there was no career, no endeavor that was off-limits to him. He could do anything and be anyone he wanted. The sky was the limit. Because Manny liked the hustle and bustle of his father's clothing business, he knew his own future was to be an entrepreneur.

When he was older, he rented a storefront on North MacQuesten Parkway in Mount Vernon, just east of Yonkers. He opened a deli and kept his eyes on the adjacent storefront, hoping to rent it, too, for additional seating. When it finally became available, he snapped it up.

Some days Manny worked twenty hours or more, keeping his business successful while casting around for more and better opportunities. He opened a second deli in the Bronx and hopped back and forth between the two. It was around this time that, on an ordinary day, he drove to a nearby deli on Locust Street in Mount Vernon to visit a friend and buy a pack of cigarettes. On his way in, he happened to notice a woman standing a few yards away on the corner of the block.

Wow, she is pretty, he thought, lingering a while before he went into the deli. *Very pretty.*

Walaa was born in Egypt to a big family of four sisters and two brothers. Her father passed away when she was young. She got married at eighteen and came to live in the United States, with dreams of opening her own hair salon. Walaa first worked in a salon in Egypt when she was thirteen, and she found that she liked it. She liked making people feel better about themselves. She even had a name all picked out for her salon: Cleopatra. The queen of Egypt, the ideal of all beauty.

After her marriage fell apart, Walaa decided to stay in Mount Vernon. She found work in a salon on Locust Street and was taking a break, standing on the corner, when she spotted a man looking at her from down the street. She looked away and then looked back. He was still there.

He's very handsome, Walaa thought.

Over the next few weeks, she would often notice the man standing outside the deli down the block, looking her way. She also noticed that she was taking more frequent breaks, expecting, maybe even hoping, to see him there. But neither Manny nor Walaa made any kind of move. The closest they came was nodding to each other from a distance on the street.

Then one morning, when Walaa had a day off, she walked into a different deli—a deli on North MacQuesten Parkway. And there, to her surprise, was Manny.

Both Manny and Walaa were caught off guard, but they smiled

at each other, as if to say, "Oh, it's you." They started talking, and the talk was easy and comfortable. They traded phone numbers and started sending texts, and eventually they agreed to go on a date to the Starbucks in Bronxville.

After that first date, they met and talked at least once a week about anything and everything, but mostly about their futures. Walaa told Manny about her plans for Cleopatra, while Manny shared his ambition to be the boss of a bunch of bustling businesses. Before long, Walaa began working part-time in Manny's deli. Neither was quick to trust other people, yet they trusted each other almost from the start. Still, they weren't quite a couple just yet.

One day, over coffee, Manny got serious.

"So you're a good hairstylist, are you?" he asked.

"Yes, I am," Walaa replied.

"Well, then why don't we open a hair salon?"

Walaa looked to see if Manny was joking. But she already knew that he wasn't. One of the things she liked about him was that when he spoke about the future, he was very serious about it. Manny was determined to succeed, and Walaa liked that because she was determined too.

"If you leave the salon and come work with me, we'll open your salon in the store next door to the deli," Manny went on. "Look, we both know what we want. We have the same goals. We want to be successful. We want to get married. We want big families. So—let's do it together."

A more formal proposal soon followed. But from that day forward, Manny and Walaa were as together as any two people could be.

Manny and Walaa got married, had two sons, and followed their dreams. Financially, it wasn't always easy—bad luck and a bad business partner forced Manny to close the deli in Mount Vernon. They sold their two cars to help finance the salon and had to borrow Manny's sister's 2006 light-blue Honda Odyssey minivan, which had about two hundred thousand miles on it. All the money they earned, they put straight into their new joint-business venture: the Cleopatra Hair Salon.

After weeks of working on the interior—new wood floors, gold-painted walls and ceiling, sleek black leather chairs, elegant chandeliers—Manny and Walaa were almost ready for the salon's grand opening. Every detail was perfect, down to the red, white, and blue bunting and balloons out front. Just a few last-minute fixes remained before the official opening in three short days.

On the morning of Tuesday, February 19, Manny dropped Walaa off at the salon, then drove the blue Odyssey up Francisco Street and turned right at the gas station onto Garfield Avenue. He was on his way to a restaurant depot to pick up supplies for the store. As soon as he turned onto Garfield, he saw a big black rat trudging slowly across the avenue, straight into traffic, a few feet in front of his van.

Manny hit the brakes and watched the rat go. As he looked closer, he could tell it wasn't a rat. No, it was a cat. Then he noticed the thing had a fluffy tail, and its tail was tucked down as it slouched slowly across the busy avenue.

That's not a cat, Manny thought. *That's a dog.*

The odd thing was, the dog seemed as if it was on a suicide mission. He was walking slowly, head down, oblivious to oncoming cars. He was forlorn, covered in dirt, his fur matted, his steps listless. As he walked, he turned and looked at Manny in the van. The dog's eyes seemed devoid of life. Luckily, both Manny and another driver stopped before they hit him, and the dog continued its mournful journey to the concrete sidewalk.

Manny put the van in park and flicked on the hazard lights. He jumped out and went over to the dog.

"Hey, buddy," Manny said. "Are you lost?"

The dog stopped, turned, and slowly walked toward Manny. Manny reached down and picked him up. The dog offered no resistance; it was as though he no longer cared what happened to him. Manny looked him over more closely. Other than a layer of dirt, he didn't look too bad off. He wasn't hurt or bleeding or anything, and dirt aside, it was obvious he'd been recently groomed. There was nothing about him that made Manny think he was a feral or junkyard dog. In fact, Manny concluded, the opposite was true.

This is somebody's dog, he thought. *Somebody loves this dog.*

Just then, a car drove by and stopped. The driver stuck his head out the window.

"You just find that dog?"

"Yeah," Manny said.

"If you don't want him, I'll take him," the man said.

Manny stood there with the dog in his arms, considering the offer. He and Walaa were way too busy to add a dog to their lives. Perhaps they'd get one down the road, but certainly not right then. There couldn't have been a worse time for them to take on that kind of responsibility. Manny could just hand the dog over to this stranger and be done with it.

Manny looked at the dog again. The dog peered up at him with big, innocent eyes. *Maybe his owner is looking for him*, Manny thought. *Maybe we won't have to keep him forever.*

"Nah, don't worry about it," Manny told the driver. "I'll hold on to him."

The Search: Day Seven
February 21

The bottom line is, I miss Oliver. I miss him when he's not around.

Even worse than missing him is knowing he is missing me. He never likes it when I leave for work. After our walks, he doesn't follow me into the cottage. Instead, he stays outside next to the car because he thinks I'm going somewhere, and he wants me to take him with me. And so, every time, I have to explain it to him.

"Daddy's got to go out," I'll say. "Daddy's got to go to work. I'm gonna leave the TV on, and you need to be a good boy, okay? Don't worry, Daddy will be back soon."

I leave the TV on because Oliver likes watching TV. Whenever he sees a dog on TV, he barks and barks, and he's gotten to where he'll recognize a commercial and start barking even before the dog appears. So when I tell him I'm going and that I'm leaving the TV on for him, Oliver marches over to his little dog bed, lies down, and looks up at me and watches me as I leave. He doesn't complain, he doesn't bark, he doesn't even budge—he just stays still and silent in his bed, as if he's saying, Don't worry, Dad, it's cool. I got this. You go. I'll be fine.

And then, as I close the cottage door and head to my car, it's like I can almost hear him think, Just come back soon, Dad, okay? Don't stay out too long.

Chapter Twenty-Four

I spent the night on Laura's sofa and woke up after nine solid hours of sleep. It was probably the best I'd slept since the ordeal began. I guess I was exhausted. The days were blending into one another, and I didn't realize that Thursday marked one full week since Oliver was taken.

The day before in Mount Vernon had been hard. Seeing the look-alike Oliver crushed our spirits. The worst part for me was feeling for the first time that my sister Laura was also starting to question why we hadn't already gotten Oliver back. She was my rock, but even she felt punched in the gut by what had happened the day before. The longer we went without Oliver, the harder it would be for either of us to pretend we truly believed we would get him back.

I got a cup of coffee from the kitchen and checked Nancy's Facebook page about Oliver. For a guy who never really got into Facebook, I'd sure found a source of comfort there, in the form of people's comments and well-wishes. There were hundreds of them. I checked the number of shares and likes, which had been growing steadily all week.

There were now more than fifteen thousand.

I took stock of this incredible wave of support. These were people from all around the country, stopping their days to pray for me and send me kind words. So many people told me that the story of Oliver made them cry, even though they didn't know me or Oliver.

I'd read a little about empathy; I knew there were scientific studies that showed we are hardwired to feel a sense of interconnectedness. We all want to be part of a group, part of one another's lives. Someone else's pain can activate our own physiological responses to suffering, so we can easily put ourselves in other people's shoes. It's almost as if we can catch emotions, just like we catch a cold.

That's what was happening now, with Oliver. People were feeling my pain. They were offering their support, praying for me, praying for sweet Oliver's return, so I would know I didn't have to endure the nightmare alone. That, of course, was *exactly* how I felt when the week began. But how could I continue to feel that way in the face of so much love and heartfelt empathy?

I read a message from a woman in Long Island. She described how she was walking her dog one afternoon when she saw someone with a dog that looked just like Oliver. "I ran up to the dog and yelled, 'Oliver!' to see if he would react to the name," she explained. "Instead, I just scared the heck out of him, and he jumped about ten feet back."

I laughed. Then I thanked the woman for looking for Oliver and for making me laugh, which was pretty hard to do.

I signed off of Facebook and told Laura I was going back to Mount Vernon. She said she was coming with me. My sister Nancy had the day off from work, and she called to say she would meet us there too.

"I don't want you two to be there alone," she said. "I cannot sit here and do nothing."

On the car ride down, I silently said a prayer, and as I did, I began to feel—I don't know—optimistic? I felt like the love from my sisters, from Facebook, from the woman with the Oliver look-alike, and from everyone who had crossed my path that week was all coming together, coming toward me and lifting me and filling me with strength. I felt newly determined. We had no plan for the day. All we could do was sit and wait. But even so, driving down the Bronx River Parkway to Mount Vernon, on a day when bright sunshine replaced the dreary clouds, I had an inkling, a tiny hint, the very beginnings of a notion that maybe, just maybe, this could be the day.

My father and I were going to the supermarket. He was pushing the shopping cart and wheezing and coughing from his emphysema. He was sixty-six years old and not doing well. The evening before, he had flown into one of his rages and screamed at me for doing something. I can't remember what it was. I didn't fight back—I'd stopped fighting back long ago. I let him rant and rave, and then I shuffled away to my bedroom.

The next morning, I felt sluggish. I was depressed. As accustomed as I had become to my father screaming at me, it was never an easy thing to absorb. It took its toll. It made me turn inward and fall silent. As we walked in the parking lot toward the supermarket, my father noticed how quiet I was, and he understood why. He could always see the damage he was causing to everyone around him. He was just powerless to stop it.

A few feet from the entrance, he stopped pushing the cart. He then turned and looked at me, and in a low, raspy voice, he said, "Steven, I'm sorry for what I did to you last night."

"It's okay, Dad."

"No, it's *not*," he said forcefully, grabbing my arm and gripping it tightly. "It's not okay."

He let go of my arm and looked away, taking a deep, labored breath.

"I don't know why I do what I do," he said. "But it's not right. I just don't know why I do it. But I'm sorry I hurt you so much. I'm really sorry, Steven."

Why did my father do the things he did? Was it a chemical imbalance? Was it because of something that happened to him during World War II? Or because of some other event from his past? Like I said, there was no real way for me to know what had shaped him into the man he became.

Whatever it was, something about my father's confession—the first time he'd ever apologized for his actions—affected me deeply. It was as if a curtain was pulled back and I finally saw my father for what he was: a human being who was suffering. A man who was in pain because of the pain he caused others. And that touched my heart because I knew my father was a good man. He meant well, and when he was sober, he could be wonderful.

I thought back to the twelfth grade, when I wrote a play for drama class called *The President's Lounge*. It was about an angel in heaven who brings eight great presidents together for a conversation. I wasn't sure it was any good, but my teacher loved it and gave me a triple A-plus along with the praise "Extraordinary!" For some reason I *did* show that grade to my father, risking his usual denigration. Instead, he was hugely complimentary, and it was obvious he was proud of me, just like he had been back at his bar when I was young and naming the presidents. I had almost forgotten there were moments—not many, but a few—when my father showed his love and pride for me and not just his disappointment.

I know that my father loved his family, but I'm not so sure how much he loved himself.

In any case, my father could never change the past, and neither could I. All each of us had was the present, the now. And the instant he apologized to me, I was able to completely forgive my father for all of his wrongdoings, not just for that day, but forever. I forgave my father for *everything*.

This surprised me. I hadn't been sure how I would react if the subject of his abuses ever came up between us. Would I express anger and bitterness? Would I lash out and tell him his apology was too little too late? No—without even thinking about it, I reacted instinctively to his confession with an immense feeling of love for him. As best he could, my father was revealing himself to me. He was laying bare his humanity. He was opening his soul. And when he did, whatever book of grievances I might have been compiling slammed shut and disintegrated in an onrush of compassion.

Were the effects of all my father's abuses suddenly, miraculously lifted? No. I didn't have the power to erase them. But I *did* have the power to forgive them. As I talked with my father outside the supermarket, I recognized the enormity of this power, and I stood in awe of it. And how it seemed to fill me up and transfer from me to my father. How it enveloped him in kindness and grace so that he wouldn't feel all alone in the world but rather understand that he was loved by his family, flaws and all. Because he was ours and we were his, and we had given him our forgiveness.

I put my hand on my father's shoulder and told him again that it was okay. We were good. We were fine. Everything was fine. Then we went into the supermarket, my father moving slowly and coughing, and we picked up some groceries and went home.

My father died a few months later, on October 21, 1988, at the age of sixty-six. Since his passing, I have visited him and my mother at St. Patrick's Cemetery in Huntington hundreds of times, just to talk to them and ask for their help, to let my mother know that I am doing okay, and to thank my father for the day he taught me the awesome power of forgiveness.

Chapter Twenty-Five

Manny put the scruffy dog in the passenger seat of the Honda Odyssey, then turned around and headed back to the Cleopatra salon. The dog immediately jumped on his lap and put his face to the window. Manny lowered the window, and the dog stuck part of his head out, savoring the sharply cold wind on his face.

Okay, this dog is car friendly, Manny thought. *For sure, he is a domestic dog. Someone owns this dog.*

Manny double-parked outside the hair salon and walked inside with the dog. Walaa looked up from what she was doing, and her mouth dropped open.

"What is that?" she asked.

"This is somebody's dog," Manny said. "I found him on Garfield Avenue. Somebody treated him well and really loves him, I can tell. But he's lost, and he's really sad."

"Okay," Walaa said, "let's put him on the chair in the back. I have a customer coming. I hope he doesn't bark."

Manny put the dog on the brown leather chair, and the dog sat there quietly and looked around.

"He must be hungry," Manny said. Then he went to a deli and picked up a quarter pound of smoked turkey. Back at the salon, he put the turkey on a paper plate and poured water into a cup. Then he put the plate and cup on a chair next to the sofa. The dog came over and ate all the turkey and drank all the water. Then he looked up at Manny and Walaa and licked his lips, as if to say thank you.

Manny remembered something someone had told him—if you feed a dog once, he will remember you for three years. Manny didn't know if that was true, but he felt he had earned the little dog's trust, and that made him feel good.

"You're gonna be just fine," he told the dog.

That evening, Manny and Walaa took the dog home with them to their apartment a few blocks away. They were in the process of moving to a new apartment just above the salon, so everything was a mess. They hadn't had any TV or internet in more than a week. They also had a new baby, two-month-old Ameer. It was a hectic time, even before the dog showed up. But what could they do now but take care of him until his rightful owner appeared?

In their apartment, Manny realized he would need to take the dog out for a walk. He didn't have a leash, so he drove to the local CVS to buy dog food and a leash. At the store, however, he couldn't find a dog collar. So when he got home, he took a small cloth baby belt and gently wrapped it around the dog's neck before hooking the leash to the belt. At first, the dog was hesitant to leave the apartment. But with a little coaxing, Manny got him down to the street. Halfway down the block, the dog did his business and then started back toward the apartment, walking so fast he tugged on the leash. *He really wants to go inside*, Manny thought. *He doesn't want to be outside anymore.*

That night, Walaa mixed some wet and dry dog food and put it on a dish on the floor of their bedroom, where their two sons were lying on the bed. Meanwhile, Manny went to another room to change out of his work clothes. When he returned, he saw the dog up on the bed, happily lying next to their two children.

"Maybe we should give him a bath," Walaa said.

Manny took the dog to the bathroom and washed him down in the tub. The dog didn't resist a bit. He wasn't too dirty, but he did smell. Manny took him out of the tub and tried to dry him with a towel. But he was still wet, so Manny used his wife's hair dryer to gently blow him dry. When he put the clean dog on the floor, the dog ran straight back to the bedroom and jumped on the bed again.

"He wants to be with the kids," Walaa said.

The dog was so quiet, well-mannered, and lovable, Manny and Walaa were both smitten fairly quickly. Walaa had had dogs before, when she was young, but they were all big and loud, and she hadn't given much thought to getting a pet as an adult. Yet there was no doubt she was already fond of the adorable dog who allowed her kids to pet him on the bed. Manny, on the other hand, had long been an animal lover, and he knew a good dog when he saw one. And this was a good dog.

Eventually it occurred to both Manny and Walaa that if the dog's owner never showed up, well, that might not be the worst thing that could happen.

"Honey," Walaa told Manny, "I think he wants to sleep in here."

Manny knew what that meant. He grabbed his pillow and slept on the sofa that night.

The next day, Walaa and Manny took turns looking after the dog. Walaa fed him and kept him company; Manny took him on his walks.

"Come on, buddy"—Manny called him buddy—"Let's go for a

walk," he'd say. "I don't know where you came from, but as long as you're here, let's go."

Really, the dog wasn't trouble at all. The big problem was finding out who owned him. They hadn't heard anything about a lost dog, nor had they seen any flyers. And without a TV or an internet connection, they had no way of learning about one. All they could do for the moment was keep the dog safe and healthy, and wait.

On their first full day with the dog, they decided to leave him alone in the apartment when they went to work in the morning. The dog didn't fight them and seemed fine with staying behind. But when Manny came home from work later, he thought the dog looked sad again. *He likes people*, Manny thought. *He needs to be around people.* If they kept him any longer, they would have to find a way not to leave him home alone for too long.

The following morning, when Manny got ready to leave at nine o'clock, the dog raced toward him and got between him and the door and started yelping, which so far he hadn't done.

"What is it, buddy?" Manny asked. "What's wrong?"

The dog kept barking, and Manny thought he knew what the dog was trying to say.

He was saying, *I wanna go! Don't leave me here! Take me, please. Please take me.*

"He wants to come with us," Walaa told Manny.

"Well, then, I guess he gets to come," Manny said.

They decided to take the dog with them on an errand and then back to the salon, where he could spend the day with Walaa. Manny got the minivan, and as Walaa loaded up the boys, the dog jumped into Manny's lap in the driver's seat. Manny rolled down the window, and the dog stuck out its head. *How about that*, Manny thought. *We already have a ritual.*

Manny drove to the restaurant depot, where he picked up more supplies. Then it was back to the salon. It was midmorning, and the traffic was bad. To avoid a jam on the route he normally took, Manny turned down Cresswell Boulevard, toward Norton Street. As he headed to the corner, he saw the traffic light ahead turn yellow. He punched the gas and tried to beat the red light. He almost made it, but at the last second, he had to hit the brakes. The van sat at the corner of Norton and Cresswell, waiting for a green light.

"Manny, look at that," Walaa said suddenly.

"Look at what?"

"That, up there. That paper on the pole."

Manny looked out his window. On the corner he saw a telephone pole, and taped to the pole was a piece of paper.

On the paper, he saw a picture of a dog.

Chapter Twenty-Six

When we got to Mount Vernon, Laura and I walked around handing out flyers. We were still feeling defeated from the day before, and then we saw that many of our flyers had been ripped down. Our moods sank even more. As we were replacing the flyers, two police officers in a squad car pulled up alongside us.

"You guys again?" one of them said.

It was the same two officers who had impounded the stolen white SUV. One of them had short, dark hair and shaved sides and wore imposing wraparound sunglasses; the other had a square jaw and a clean-cut, all-American appearance. They were both smiling, surprised, apparently, to see us still in Mount Vernon, still searching for Oliver.

"We're not leaving without my dog," I told them.

They both smiled.

"You're gonna be able to run for mayor of this town if you keep working the streets every day," the dark-haired officer said with a laugh. "Just be careful."

The officers drove off, and Laura and I sat in her car, strategically parked outside the redbrick building. Not much later, Nancy arrived from Brooklyn and joined us in the car.

There wasn't much for us to do but wait. Wait for something good to happen. The last few days, we'd never given a thought to when or where we would eat. We just grabbed food when we could, usually at the end of a long day. This wasn't the healthiest way to go about anything, so I asked my sisters if they were hungry. They said they were. For once, we were going to have something resembling a proper breakfast.

I walked to the corner deli and ordered three egg sandwiches and three coffees. The woman behind the counter looked at me and asked, "You're the guy with the stolen dog, right?" I told her that I was.

"That kid was in here the other day trying to sell the dog," she said.

"Yeah, I know. I came in here that day."

"Yeah, but you came in right after he was here. You don't know how close you were to getting your dog back."

I smiled wistfully. I'd been really close to finding Oliver a few times. But I was always just a minute or two too late.

"You know what?" I told the woman. "This is a really wonderful community. Really nice people."

"We have a bad reputation," she said. "But once you're in the community, you see that everyone's got your back."

She put the sandwiches and coffee cups in two cardboard holders, and I carried them back to where we were parked. In Laura's car we tore into our sandwiches, which were delicious. The top of Laura's dashboard was soon covered with wrappings, coffee-cup lids, stirrers, and napkins.

"We're like detectives," I said.

"Yeah, detectives on a stakeout," Laura said.

"Yeah, like Kojak."

My cell phone chimed. The number was unfamiliar. Over the

week I'd received a number of calls that turned out to be either well-wishers or false leads, so I no longer got excited by calls. Still, we took every tip and lead seriously.

It was a little before noon when I answered the phone.

"Hello?"

"Hello, is this Steven?"

"Yes, I'm Steven. Who is this?"

"My name is Manny. I'm calling to see, uh . . . are you missing a dog?"

At the corner of Norton Street and Cresswell Boulevard, Manny stepped out of the blue Odyssey to get a closer look at the flyer on the telephone pole. He pulled it down from the pole and took it back to the van.

"I think it's him," he told Walaa.

The dog was now snuggled on Walaa's lap, and she was holding him tightly.

"How do you know?"

"I don't know, but it looks like him."

"Yeah, but it might not be him. We can't just hand him over to anybody."

"The only way to know is to call the guy. Let me call the guy."

Manny pulled the van into a parking spot. He took out his cell and entered the number on the flyer. After two rings, a man picked up. Manny asked him if he was Steven and if he was missing a dog. The man said he was.

"I have a dog right here," Manny said. "He is black, like the dog in the picture. I don't know; it looks like him."

Manny heard two female voices asking Steven who was calling.

"Shhhh, hold on, hold on," Manny heard Steven tell them. "This guy says he has a dog. He says he has Oliver."

"Wait a minute," Manny said. "Is that your dog's name? Oliver? That's his name?"

"Yes, that's his name. His name is Oliver."

"Okay, wait a minute. Let me try something."

Manny turned to the little dog on Walaa's lap. The dog looked back with big wide eyes.

"Oliver?" Manny said to the dog. "Are you Oliver?"

The dog jumped up and down and wagged his tail and barked and spun in a circle and otherwise went dog crazy.

Manny looked at Walaa. Now they knew.

It was the first time Oliver had heard his name in a week.

"Listen, I think I have your dog," the man on the phone told me. "I said his name, and he is going crazy."

The sensation that came over me in that instant was a mix of sheer exhilaration and disbelief. I felt shot through with adrenaline, and nothing seemed real. I had to force myself to be in the moment and not get ahead of myself.

"Where are you?" I nearly shouted into the phone.

"We're headed toward North MacQuesten Parkway."

"What? Where is that? How do you spell it?"

Nancy and Laura dug around frantically for a pen. They couldn't find one. The half-eaten egg sandwiches were everywhere.

"Who is he? What's he saying?" Laura asked.

"Shhh, I can't hear him."

"Put the call on speaker," Laura said.

I put the call on speaker.

"Hold on, let me FaceTime you," Manny told me. "I'll put the dog on camera if I can get him to sit still."

I switched to FaceTime and stared at the phone. A man came into view—Manny. The image blurred as he moved the phone around. Finally, it stabilized, and a dog was in the frame. The dog was sitting on a woman's lap. I looked at the dog and blinked three or four times. Time stopped.

"Oh my God!" I shouted. "That's Oliver! It's him, it's him, it's Oliver!"

"Let me see! Let me look," my sisters said.

I handed my phone to Laura.

"Tell me it's him," I said. "Tell me it's him. Is that him?"

"It looks like him," Laura said.

"Nancy, is it him? Tell me it's him."

"It could be him," Nancy said. "It really looks like him."

"It's Oliver, right? It's him. Is it him?"

Both Laura and Nancy reached their conclusions at the same time.

"That's Oliver," they said.

They handed me the phone, and I looked at the dog again. I locked eyes with him. Oliver is one of those dogs who can read screens well. He always recognizes dogs on TV. Could he see me through the iPhone screen and understand it was me? Could he recognize me this way?

I will never know for sure, but as we looked at each other through the tiny screen, I truly believed he was thinking, *There's Stee! There's Stee! I knew he was coming! I knew it!*

"That's Oliver!" I screamed at Manny. "That's my Oliver."

Manny knew he'd found the dog's owner. The dog's uncontainable excitement at the voice on the other end of the phone was the clincher. Walaa knew it, too, and she was relieved, but also, if she was being honest, disappointed. The dog—Oliver—had really grown on her and her sons. She'd been caring for him for less than two days, but already he'd wormed his way into their hearts. Walaa knew she was going to miss him.

"Where are you?" I asked. "Where are you *right now*?"

"Hold on. Let me look around," Manny said. "I'm on Cresswell Boulevard."

"Oh my God, I know where Cresswell Boulevard is!" I said. "It's right down the block from me. I'm looking at it right now!"

"Wait a minute, so you're right here?" Manny said.

"Do me a favor. Hold up your phone," I said. "Hold it up in the air."

Manny held up the phone and let me see the store on the corner—a bar called the Blue Raccoon. The store's sign featured two images of blue raccoons. I saw the two raccoons, and I knew I had seen them before. I had walked by that sign before. In fact, I knew exactly where it was: it was at the end of the very block where I was standing.

"You're down the street!" I yelled into the phone. "You're right here. Nancy, Laura, he's right down the block. Oliver is right down the block!"

To Manny, I yelled, "Stay where you are!"

I jumped out of Laura's car, my egg sandwich and coffee jumping out with me and spilling to the curb. My sisters and I were a flurry of arms and legs. I didn't wait for them—I took off running down the block. If a man can fly, well then, I believe I flew down that street. For a brief moment in my fifty-five years of living, I was finally the baseball hero rounding third base in game seven of the World Series, bursting with speed, madly dashing for victory, the crowd cheering for me to "Run!"

For a few brief seconds I had wings, and my feet barely touched the ground.

As I neared the corner of Norton, I strained to see Manny or Oliver. All I could see was a big blue minivan. It was parked on the corner, across the street from the Blue Raccoon, alongside a grassy, fenced-in lot marked "Tupelo Equipment." I ran to the van, completely out of breath. And then I felt my knees nearly give out.

Because the passenger-side door of the van was open, and a woman was sitting inside the van, and on her lap was . . . my sweet, wonderful, beautiful little boy.

He jumped from Walaa's lap straight into my arms. I held him and staggered backward, falling against the chain-link fence, and I let my body slump to the sidewalk. I squeezed Oliver and buried my face in his hair and cried. My crying was loud and shrill. My sisters Laura and Nancy came around the corner shouting Oliver's name. I didn't want to let go of him, but I knew he had to breathe, so I loosened my grip and he wiggled away, shook his body, and jumped right back in my arms. I sat up against the fence and cradled Oliver and just stared at him. I felt myself return to the land of the living. I felt my life go from black and white to color. I held my little warm ball of life, and I felt my mother and father there on the sidewalk with me in this moment of victory, just as they had been in my time of defeat.

I felt God lift me up so I could finally stand.

Oliver was home. Oliver was home. Oliver was home.

Chapter Twenty-Seven

The corner of Norton and Cresswell became a busy place. Two women in a car drove by, and when they saw me sitting on the sidewalk with Oliver, they screeched to a stop.

"Is that Oliver?" one of them yelled.

"Yes, I got him back!"

"Oh my goodness, I can't believe it! We've been following your story. We're so happy for you!"

Next, a woman we spoke to on Norton Street three days earlier, Gina, walk past. Gina's friendliness early on had really lifted our spirits and set the tone for the kindness we found in Mount Vernon. Now she got to see the incredible reunion for herself.

"God bless you," she said, tears in her eyes. "God bless you and Oliver."

Two more women came running out of the salon on the corner. They'd been following the story, too, and they started crying as well. Two days earlier, four young teenagers had helped us search the neighborhood for Oliver. They walked by the corner and stopped to celebrate, whooping it up and high-fiving each other. A young man who was down on his luck and to whom I'd given some money came by and earnestly shook my hand. Even the two police officers we met on our first day in Mount Vernon walked over to see what the commotion was about, then stuck around and posed for pictures with us. They were smiling as widely as everyone else, and they told us they had spent the morning looking around for Oliver.

"I told you I wasn't leaving until we got him!" I said to them.

A little later, Gina returned and handed me a little present for Oliver. It was a small wooden birdcage she'd built herself and inscribed, "To Oliver, God Bless Your Heart."

It was a spontaneous outpouring of love, support, and happiness. Cars driving by honked their horns, and nearly every person who passed had heard of Oliver and stopped to say hello. Laura called Lisa Reyes at News 12, and within an hour they had a crew at the scene. We filmed the happy resolution to our story. Manny and Walaa were interviewed, and they described their remarkable role in rescuing Oliver.

In all that time, I didn't let Oliver out of my arms. Nor did he wiggle or squirm or otherwise ask to be let down. Neither of us was in any hurry to be separated again, even by just a few feet.

The commotion finally died down, and I hugged Manny and Walaa and thanked them profusely for what they had done. I made sure to get their phone numbers and told them I would return soon because I wanted to give them some of the reward money. Then Laura, Nancy, and I walked back to the car. I noticed Terry and Rolando outside their shop. I went over to show them Oliver and gave them each $200 for their help.

"I'm very happy for you, brother," Rolando said. "I told you Oliver was alive."

Then I noticed a woman looking down at us through the window of her apartment in the redbrick building.

It was Donna. When she saw me with Oliver, she smiled.

"I'm very happy for you," she said.

I felt my eyes well up with tears.

"Thank you," I said. "Thank you for everything. Good luck to you. We are going home now."

Later on, someone showed me a photo they took of Oliver and me right after I got him back. The first thing I noticed was the time stamp on the photo—it was exactly noon. I immediately thought of the Sutton Clock Tower in Bedford, and how the bell had chimed so beautifully at exactly midnight.

"We have to trust in the things that happen as happening for a reason," Lucy's husband, Alan, had told me. He was right. The world is more mysterious, and more miraculous, than we can ever know.

The three of us drove to Laura's house and threw ourselves a little party. My friend Eric and his girlfriend, Lisa, came over to share in the celebration. I examined Oliver head to toe, looking for injuries, and he seemed perfectly fine. Manny and Walaa had obviously treated him well, and so, apparently, had Del and his family. In Laura's living room, I put Oliver on the floor to try and gauge his psychological state—would he run and hide? Would he flinch? Would he seem browbeaten?

A dog toy Oliver liked to play with at Laura's house was on the floor by the sofa.

"Oliver, go get your toy!" I said. "Go get it."

Oliver pranced straight to the toy and brought it over, his movements and demeanor as familiar to me as my own. We were picking up right where we left off.

Every few minutes, one of us would say how we couldn't quite believe Oliver was there with us. Even when I had Oliver on my lap, part of me couldn't accept that he was actually back. It had been so, so long since I'd held him or even looked at his face, and now that he was with me, it didn't seem real. I had to give Oliver a little squeeze now and then just to make sure he wouldn't disappear in a puff of smoke.

Nancy updated her Facebook page with the good news. By then, her post had been seen by nearly ninety thousand people. Not much later, I got a text message. It was from Helen, the young girl who'd cried when Oliver was taken.

"I heard you got Oliver back!" she wrote. "Congratulations. I'm so happy for you both!"

I took a picture of Oliver and me on Laura's sofa and sent it to her, thanking her for being there to comfort me in one of the darkest moments of my life.

Then I sent the same picture of Oliver and me to Isabela, the young woman whose wisdom changed my life the night I drove her to Bard College in the snow.

"We got him back!" I wrote.

"I am SO happy for you!" she wrote back.

I made a bunch of calls that day. To my friend Tony. To Uncle Pat. To Lucy and Alan. To everyone who stepped forward out of love and kindness and literally kept me from collapsing in a heap. When I finally had a free moment, I took Oliver out to Laura's backyard, and I thanked my mother and father and brother up above.

"I'm sorry I said the things I said to you. I should never have doubted you. I should have known you would be there for me when I needed you most."

And then I had a little talk with God.

I remembered a day from seven years earlier, when I was very close to rock bottom, living in Lucy's cottage and trying to pick up the pieces of another failed relationship—really, a failed *life*. On that day, I was bone tired of being who I was. Of being lonely and poor and unhappy. Of not having lived up to my early promise. Of continually trying to reinvent myself and always ending up with the same person—Steven the loser. I was simply sick and tired of living like that. So I went out on Lucy's driveway, looked skyward, and talked to God.

"I'm through trying to be whatever person I have been trying to be because, obviously, I'm doing something wrong," I said to him. "I want you to take over. I'm not giving up. I'm just surrendering to you. I am done trying to fulfill whatever expectations I thought I had to fulfill. I want *you* to make me into the person I am supposed to be."

I likened myself to an old block of wood with twenty coats of paint on it, all different colors. The real me was buried beneath layers and layers of paint I'd put on myself throughout the decades, as I tried desperately to become someone new. Now I needed God to strip me all the way down to that raw piece of wood. I knew it would be painful. I knew it would probably take a long time. But I needed God to make me into someone my mother could be proud of.

It was this surrender of myself to God that led me to Proverbs 3 and, ultimately, to the seven days that had just passed—both the worst and greatest week of my life.

When Oliver was stolen, the horror and misery of his loss sent me back to my old way of thinking—that God had let me down, that this was my destiny as a Carino, that I would never see Oliver again. Here was my chance to put Proverbs 3 into practice—after weeks and weeks of memorizing it on my walks with Mickey and Oliver—and instead I disregarded it.

"Trust in the LORD with all your heart and lean not on your own understanding," says verse 5. Instead, I distrusted the Lord and leaned on my old beliefs about who I was and the world around me.

"Have no fear of sudden disaster or of the ruin that overtakes the wicked, for the Lord will be at your side and will keep your foot from being snared" says verses 25 and 26. Instead, I was crippled by the disaster and believed the Lord had abandoned me—and thus, my foot *was* snared.

But my ordeal lasted for seven days, and in that time, things changed. In that time, I was given many gifts—the gift of kindness, of community, of love. In that time, many different people from all walks of life crossed my path and changed my way of thinking. Friends reminded me I was loved; strangers shared my pain. A single block in a challenged neighborhood became my world, and I saw that this world was beautiful. Words of wisdom came from everywhere, filling my heart.

And in the end, the hatred and resentment I was harboring disappeared, replaced by love and compassion. Distrust gave way to trust. The coats of paint were stripped and sanded away. Losing Oliver allowed me to live again.

This is what I thanked God for in Laura's backyard—not for returning Oliver to me but for putting me through the trial of my life and giving me the wisdom to get through it.

For giving me the mountain and helping me climb it.

That evening, Laura and Nancy and I sat in Laura's living room and had some coffee. Oliver sat happily in my lap. On the mantle, the candle Laura lit for Oliver several days earlier flickered in the dim light. Laura told me that she'd always been careful to blow it out whenever she left the house and then relight it when she came back. But that morning, she'd forgotten to blow it out when she left to join me in Mount Vernon. So the candle had burned all day.

"And just like that," I said, "we got Oliver back."

At that moment, the candle suddenly went out. Laura and Nancy and I looked at each other.

"Thanks, Mom," we all said.

That night, I curled up on Laura's sofa, and Oliver jumped up and snuggled next to me, in the hollow between my legs and my arms, and we both fell fast asleep and didn't wake up until the sun had risen.

Chapter Twenty-Eight

A few days later, Oliver and I were back in Mount Vernon.

The occasion was a gathering to celebrate the happy ending to our story. The place was the Cleopatra Hair Salon, which was now proudly open to the public.

It was my sister Nancy's suggestion to have a party there, and Manny and Walaa readily agreed. They were both profoundly affected by the roles they played in returning Oliver to me, and they wanted to be part of the celebration. We expected ten or twelve people to show up. More than forty wound up coming.

It was an amazing event. My sisters were there, along with some of their friends who had followed the story. My pals Eric and Tony showed up, and Lucy and Alan, and Janice Connolly. Some Mount Vernon residents popped in to say hello, and even some Facebook friends stopped by. So many people brought lovely little presents for Oliver. The mayor of Mount Vernon, who heard about our story, arrived and stayed for a long while, happy to talk about the kind, caring people of his city. Oliver ran around the salon and munched on some of the hors d'oeuvres we set out. He sat in a few laps and acted thrilled to be around so many people who knew his name and beamed at the sight of him.

At some point I picked up Oliver and stood at the top of the small staircase at the back of the salon, looking down on the activity below. Then I gave a little speech. I thanked everyone for coming, and I gave a thumbnail description of the events of the week. I talked about all the beautiful people I'd met in Mount Vernon and the many ways my time in the community had changed me. I read some passages from Proverbs 3. And I talked about what my friend Eric had told me when I was really down—that I was like George Bailey from *It's a Wonderful Life*.

"George Bailey got to see what life would have been like if he hadn't been born," I said. "I got to see what my life would be like without Oliver. But I also got to see how loved I am. I was given the gift of witnessing the love and support of my family, friends, clients, strangers, and, of course, the citizens of Mount Vernon. And I am extremely grateful for that. I feel the same way George Bailey felt at the end of the movie. I feel like I am the richest man in town."

A few days before the event, I'd returned to Mount Vernon to divide the reward money between Janice Connolly and Manny and Walaa. They all refused to accept it at first, but I insisted. At the Cleopatra Hair Salon during the party, Walaa came over and asked me to walk with her to the front of the store. We stood by the big window, and Walaa pointed at something out on the street. I saw a bright red Jeep parked in front of the salon.

"That is what you did for us, Steven," she said.

Manny and Walaa had used the reward money I gave them to finally get their own car, a used but shiny red Jeep with *way* fewer than two hundred thousand miles on it.

I started to tear up again, as I had a few times that day. The love and affection I felt in that room were overwhelming. For so long I'd confined myself to a solitary existence in my little one-room cottage. Now, to feel such a warm embrace from so many people—to be given, in essence, a new life in the world—seemed like a blessing of extraordinary, miraculous abundance. I found I didn't have the words to properly express the gratitude I felt. Instead, I cried a lot.

I guess I could say life returned to normal for Oliver and me, but that wouldn't really be true. For me, nothing was ever normal again, or at least not the "normal" I knew. I felt like I'd been transformed by what happened over those seven days in February. The world around me hadn't changed, but the way I looked at it had.

Getting Oliver back produced a swirl of emotions, and perhaps the most powerful one was gratitude. I wanted to say the sincerest thank you to everyone who took time out of their lives to lend me an ear or a word of support when I needed it most. So the day after we found Oliver, I brought him back to the strip mall in Scarsdale—the scene of the crime but also a scene of great kindness.

Laura came with me because we also had to take down our flyers now that Oliver was back. Our first stop was the China Buffet. The hostess who'd been so gracious about letting us put up flyers was genuinely elated to see Oliver in my arms, and she invited us in and brought the whole staff up to say hello. I thanked her for her compassion, and I told her it meant more to me than she could possibly know.

We went into the hair salon, the cigar store, the deli, and finally the Pet Goods store, where I bought Oliver a little black-and-white tuxedo shirt and a "lucky" dog biscuit. In every store, someone was moved to tears by how our ordeal had turned out. And I cried along with them.

There were many touching moments over the next few days.

Most of them were moments between just Oliver and me—our first walk together on East Field Drive, our first trip together into town, the first time he sat in my lap while I watched TV. Not a single mundane moment passed without me feeling grateful for it.

One night, I had to bartend an event for a Jewish congregation in Scarsdale. To my surprise, the host introduced me as "the man who got his dog back." The crowd cheered, and I was given a special gift, a beautiful dog bed for Oliver. It turned out that members of the congregation had followed my story on Facebook and seen my reunion with Oliver on News 12. A roomful of people I'd never met were somehow sharing in the profound joy I felt in having Oliver back.

One of the most emotional moments for me was my first trip back to the gym. After changing into my workout clothes, I lay on a foam mat and began to stretch. I had my earphones in, and I was listening to music. Suddenly it struck me that these simple things I was doing were each a little miracle. I could work out again, and I could play my beloved music again, and in fact I could live my life again—all things I was certain I had lost. But now, like Oliver, I had them back. Just then, the song "Cruel to Be Kind" by Nick Lowe came on. It was my brother Frankie's favorite song. I lay on the mat and cried, and anyone who saw me just then might have thought I was a very sad man, but they would have been wrong.

As the days passed, I thought less and less about the actual events of that fateful week—the false leads and crushing setbacks, the lucky coincidences, all the things that had to go right for me to get Oliver back. But one thought kept pushing its way into my brain, and after a while I could no longer ignore it.

So two weeks after finding Oliver, I bundled him into my car and together we went back to Mount Vernon.

I'd been thinking a lot about the kid in the baseball cap.

I really didn't know much about him, other than that he had a bad rap in the neighborhood. I knew his mother was struggling to keep him on the straight and narrow. I also knew he created the worst crisis of my adult life.

But then I began to wonder—had he also created his *own* worst crisis that week? Was stealing Oliver routine and easy for him, or had he crossed some kind of line? Perhaps Del had taken Oliver to give to his mother as a Valentine's Day gift, which would mean that he had a good heart. I also suspected he'd grown to like Oliver, and that, too, gave me a glimpse of his humanity. What if that week had been a turning point for him? What if, like me, he drew some valuable life lessons from what had happened?

Del, the kid in the baseball cap, came into my life and unwittingly played a huge part in my transformation. But what if I was also supposed to play a part in his?

Del gave me his email address when we first spoke in his apartment, and a few days after getting Oliver back, I sent him an email. I told him I hoped we might be able to get together and talk. I had no idea what I would say to him if we did meet; basically, I was following my gut. But the email bounced back to me. I sent him a few more, and they all bounced back. I figured he'd given me a phony email, which left me only one choice if I wanted to see him—go back to Norton Street.

I took the Hutchinson River Parkway from Bedford to Mount Vernon and headed straight for the redbrick building. I found a spot across from it, picked up Oliver, and went out for a walk on the block. Within minutes, I heard someone call my name.

"Steven!"

It was Derek, Janice Connolly's husband. The guy who'd told us where Del lived. He came over and gave me a hug and asked how I was doing.

"Pretty great now," I said, pointing to Oliver.

"I'm happy you guys found each other," he said.

A short while later, I heard my name again. It was Rolando the mechanic. He gave me a hug too. Then a man who'd asked me for change on my first day in Mount Vernon walked by and recognized me. This time, he didn't ask for money; instead, he smiled and shook my hand. Two other people I remembered from my three days in Mount Vernon came over to say hello and pet Oliver and smile and tell me how happy they were that I finally had him back.

I'd never felt so welcomed by a community in my whole life.

I kept an eye out for Del, but he never appeared. I didn't want to go up to his apartment and bother his family again; I was just hoping to run into him. Something told me I was going to see him that day. So Oliver and I sat together on the front stoop of the redbrick building and waited.

Within minutes, Del walked out.

He saw me and broke into a big smile. Then he saw Oliver and reached down and gently patted him on the head.

"Hi, Oliver," he said.

"Del, it's good to see you," I told him. "I was trying to reach you. I sent you emails, but they all bounced back."

"Oh, yeah?" he said. "That's funny. It should be working."

"Okay," I said. "I'll try again."

"Yeah, try again."

"So how are you doing, Del?"

"I'm good. I'm okay."

"That's good to hear. I really wanted to know how you were doing."

Then we fell into silence. I didn't know what more to say; I didn't even know what I was doing there. What was my plan? What had I expected? Del and I were from two different worlds. We couldn't know each other's lives or experiences. We weren't close in age, and we didn't live in the same place. We weren't part of the same community.

Or were we?

Weren't we both a part of the special community created by Oliver?

"I gotta go," Del finally said.

"Listen, before you go—I just, I just wanted us to talk," I said. "Just talk sometime, you know?"

"Okay," he said.

"Okay then. I'll email you again. And maybe we can get together sometime."

Del smiled and shook my hand. Then he started walking away.

A few steps down the street, he turned and gave Oliver and me a little wave.

"Talk to you later," he said.

"Yeah, definitely, talk later," I said.

And I meant it. I knew right then that I would see Del again, and I knew what I wanted to do for him. If he would allow me, I wanted to take him to an animal rescue and get him his own dog. Maybe he would say no. Maybe he hadn't really fallen in love with Oliver, like I suspected. But something told me he might say yes. And if he did, then he'd come to realize what I already knew—dogs make us better humans. They bring out the best in us.

Conclusion

What would Oliver have thought as he sat in the van with Manny and Walaa and heard my voice come over the cell phone? What about when he heard Manny ask him if his name was Oliver? What would he have thought in those amazing few seconds?

He would have thought, *That's Stee. I knew he was near. I knew he would come get me.* And then he would have used his communicative skills to emphasize the connection: barking, spinning, unmistakable elation.

And when he finally saw me turn the corner on Cresswell Boulevard, come toward him in the van, and get close enough for him to jump through the air into my arms—what would he have been thinking then?

He would have been thinking, *I know this smell. I know this sound. I know this face. This is Stee. This is my human. And now, he is here.*

I know he would have been thinking these things because, as I said, I believe Oliver and I understand each other's thoughts. But it's not just me who believes that. All over the planet, animal cognition scientists are doing canine neuroimaging research that proves dogs are as obsessed with us as we are with them. They depend on us for sustenance, but no more than we depend on them for love and companionship. Dogs are closer to their humans than they are to even one another. So when our little friends give us endless affection and make us think, *Gee, they really love us*, it's because they do.

The connection is ancient and heartfelt.

This is how I know that when Oliver and I endured our separate week of drama and anxiety and fear, deep down Oliver would have been thinking, *Stee and I are not apart. We're just not together right now.*

He would have understood this impermeable connection even better than I did.

Of course, during that same week, I also experienced a loss of connection with God. I felt abandoned by him, and thus I felt that he had torn us apart. But I was wrong. God never abandoned me. He was always right there with me. He tried to tell me this through Proverbs 3:5: "Trust in the LORD with all your heart and lean not on your own understanding"—and I thought I'd absorbed the lesson, but really I hadn't.

So he taught it to me again, in Mount Vernon.

"Nothing ever becomes real till it is experienced," the English poet John Keats once wrote. Well, even a proverb is just a saying until it is actualized in your life. That is what happened to me. I learned the true lesson of Proverbs 3 by living it, and that was God's great gift to me.

I don't know what the future holds for Oliver, or for Del, or for me. Will there be more hardships and setbacks? Probably. To be alive means to face just such tests all the time. Going forward, will I be able to see these tests as blessings from God? I sure hope I will.

What I do know for certain is that as long as I face these tests using God's tools—wisdom, understanding, compassion, love—I won't be alone in the fight.

We are all part of a community. Geographic communities,

spiritual communities, even accidental communities—there is always something that binds us to one another. Which means that none of us is ever truly alone. I believe this now.

It's written on the tablet of my heart.

Proverbs 3

My son, do not forget my teaching,
but keep my commands in your heart,
for they will prolong your life many years
and bring you peace and prosperity.

Let love and faithfulness never leave you;
bind them around your neck,
write them on the tablet of your heart.
Then you will win favor and a good name
in the sight of God and man.
Trust in the Lord with all your heart
and lean not on your own understanding;
in all your ways submit to him,
and he will make your paths straight.

Do not be wise in your own eyes;
fear the Lord and shun evil.
This will bring health to your body
and nourishment to your bones.

Honor the LORD with your wealth,
with the firstfruits of all your crops;
then your barns will be filled to overflowing,
and your vats will brim over with new wine.

My son, do not despise the LORD's discipline,
and do not resent his rebuke,
because the LORD disciplines those he loves,
as a father the son he delights in.

Blessed are those who find wisdom,
those who gain understanding,
for she is more profitable than silver
and yields better returns than gold.
She is more precious than rubies;
nothing you desire can compare with her.
Long life is in her right hand;
in her left hand are riches and honor.
Her ways are pleasant ways,
and all her paths are peace.
She is a tree of life to those who take hold of her;
those who hold her fast will be blessed.

By wisdom the LORD laid the earth's foundations,
by understanding he set the heavens in place;
by his knowledge the watery depths were divided,
and the clouds let drop the dew.

My son, do not let wisdom and understanding out of your sight,
preserve sound judgment and discretion;
they will be life for you,
an ornament to grace your neck.

Then you will go on your way in safety,
and your foot will not stumble.
When you lie down, you will not be afraid;
when you lie down, your sleep will be sweet.
Have no fear of sudden disaster
or of the ruin that overtakes the wicked,
for the LORD will be at your side
and will keep your foot from being snared.

Do not withhold good from those to whom it is due,
when it is in your power to act.
Do not say to your neighbor,
"Come back tomorrow and I'll give it to you"—
when you already have it with you.
Do not plot harm against your neighbor,
who lives trustfully near you.
Do not accuse anyone for no reason—
when they have done you no harm.

Do not envy the violent
or choose any of their ways.

For the LORD detests the perverse
but takes the upright into his confidence.
The LORD's curse is on the house of the wicked,
but he blesses the home of the righteous.
He mocks proud mockers
but shows favor to the humble and oppressed.
The wise inherit honor,
but fools get only shame.

Acknowledgments

The story of Oliver is a gift. It is a true story about the power of faith.

By my door, as I exit my cottage, I have a small wooden plaque that reminds me every day of what the definition of faith is: "Understanding is the reward of faith. Therefore, seek not to understand that you may believe, but believe that you may understand."—St. Augustine (354–430)

I would like to first acknowledge the power of faith, which is to give thanks to God, my parents, and my brother, Frank. Yes, there were many things we, the living, did correctly in getting Oliver back, but I believe that the unseen forces also played a major role in essentially saving my life. That's just who I am, how I think, and what I believe. So, to those whom we cannot see, thank you for giving me the two most important virtues a person could ask for—wisdom and understanding.

In the world in which we can see and touch, I must thank quite a few people who made this story possible. First, is my cowriter, Alex Tresniowski. Your talent and skill as a heartfelt writer is second to none. You have taken my story, my words, and made them beautiful and emotional. It has been an honor to be associated with you on this book.

Where would I be without my sisters? Laura, to say you came

to the aid of your little brother is an understatement. Your determination to get Oliver back was incredible. You have been there before—during my many trials in life—as someone to talk to, confide in, and depend on. This was THE mountain of all trials. I could have never climbed it without you. Thank you for never giving up on Oliver or me.

Nor would there be a happy ending without my sister Nancy. Determined to spread the word via social media, you did it with precision and force. You had thousands of shares and views on your posts, and that support kept me going. You made several trips from Brooklyn to do whatever you could for me, and I am grateful for your support and love. To have you and Laura with me when Oliver jumped into my arms was a moment I will never forget.

My oldest sister Annette Lubsen could not participate in our pet detective work because she lives in Florida. But I know if you lived in New York, you would have been in the car with us the day we got Oliver back. We felt your prayers, from you and your husband, Bruce, every day.

I received many calls that week from my family who were desperately hoping I would find Oliver. I would like to thank John Johansen, Nancy's husband, and their two children: Jena and Christian for their support. My sister Annette's children: my niece Colette Reid and her husband, Mike; my niece Brooke Cassens and her husband, Steve; and my nephew Derek Lubsen and his wife, Brook. Thank you for your calls, texts, and notes of support during the most difficult week of my life.

My Uncle Pat and Aunt Rita, who live in Delaware, thank you for your generosity at a most difficult time in my life. Your support, both monetarily and emotionally, gave my sisters and me a huge boost in our search efforts.

Where would my story be without a literary agent who believed in it? Nena Madonia Oshman of Dupree Miller was that person. We submitted a proposal to her, and on my way back from the cemetery in Huntington where I often go to see my parents and brother, she called. Her voice, filled with excitement, said two words that I will never forget: "this story is precious and timeless." Thank you, Nena and Jan Miller, for believing in me, and the story of Oliver.

Where would my story be without a publisher who believed in it as well? Thomas Nelson, a division of HarperCollins Christian Publishing is that publisher. From day one, they have treated my story with the utmost respect. Thank you, Jessica Wong (associate publisher) for listening to me practically cry on the phone as I told you my story. To Brigitta Nortker (senior editor), who answered all my questions so patiently; both of you, your comments have been very uplifting and supportive. To the other professionals who have taken time to proofread and edit my book, Whitney Bak (copyeditor), Jennifer Lonas and Nat Akin (proofreaders), thank you.

A special thank you to Kristina Juodenas (art director: cover). Need I say more? What a spectacular cover design. And thank you, Phoebe Wetherbee (designer: interior) for *Oliver*. You added so many wonderful touches to the book.

I would like to thank Shaina Fishman (commercial photographer) for taking such beautiful photos of Oliver. The cover of the book is stunning, and you captured his essence perfectly!

A special mention to Lorraine Stundis (photographer); my author photo with Oliver was taken about three months after our being reunited in Mount Vernon. You captured the essence of our happiness together, with Oliver literally smiling! You took so many beautiful photos that day. Thank you.

A beautiful book needs a marketing team to make things happen,

ACKNOWLEDGMENTS

and once again, *Oliver*, was placed in the hands of true professionals. Thank you to the marketing team—Rachel Tockstein (marketing manager), Karen Jackson (senior director of marketing), Claire Drake (marketing associate), and Sara Broun (director of publicity).

There were many key players in holding me together during that fateful week. To Lucy Galasso and Alan McCollom, thank you for your support. Lucy, for coming to Mount Vernon with us, and Alan, for the talk that most difficult Friday evening, and for the pizza delivery on that cold Tuesday night! I have lived in your cottage for nearly nine years, and what incredible lessons I have learned through a simpler life.

Lisa Reyes at News 12, Westchester, thank you for showing up not once, but twice! Your interview with me that Friday was simply incredible. We called you, and you showed up with your cameraman in an hour. We called you again when we got Oliver back, and there you were, in Mount Vernon, to celebrate our happiest moment. I am forever grateful to you and News 12 for all the attention you gave our story.

To Eric Weinstein, my friend. We have gone from stuffing newspapers as teenagers, to bartending as grown men, to that dismal Saturday when you came to my rescue to provide me with support. You are a friend indeed. I'll never forget it. I am glad you and Lisa could celebrate Oliver's return with my family!

Tony Marcogliese, you came to our aid on that Tuesday and stayed with us all day and night. Your sudden arrival in Mount Vernon was much needed and appreciated by both me and my sister Laura. Thank you for caring so much about Oliver and me.

Thank you, Isabela Dunlap, for a conversation that turned the tide of our story from bitterness to love. Your compassion and patience with me that evening was exactly what I needed. You spoke from the heart, and those words entered my heart, and your comforting words changed my attitude in my search for Oliver.

Janice Connolly, thank you for taking the picture of Oliver that led us to Mount Vernon. Your small act of kindness ignited this story. It should never be forgotten how one small act of kindness can indeed change the world. You did just that.

Manny and Walaa, thank you for taking care of my Oliver. Manny, you rescued him from the street, and Walaa, even though you had two young children to attend to, you took in Oliver and cared for him like he was one of your own. God bless both of you for bringing this story to fruition. You saved my life with your kindness.

Rolando and Terry, the mechanics who helped keep me sane while I climbed fences, walked on rooftops, and searched high and low for Oliver. Thank you for caring about us and showing us the window of support that Mount Vernon gave all of us.

A special thank you to the citizens of Mount Vernon, New York. You let us scour your streets, searching frantically for my Oliver, and offered nothing but kindness. There was no judgment or questioning of our motives. Thank you for treating us with respect and dignity at all times. Maybe that is why Mount Vernon is called "The City of Hope."

There were people I have met along this road, some current, some from years ago, that mysteriously played their own role in the story of Oliver. Mr. Adams, my fourth-grade teacher, for instance, made a difference by simply caring enough to get me Harry S. Truman's address. His letter hangs on my wall today as a reminder of who I once thought I could be. Thank you, Mr. Adams, for caring. You created one of the most cherished moments I ever had with my mother.

Through a series of unfortunate choices and events, I was pretty much washed up in 2011 when I got my driving job at Armonk

ACKNOWLEDGMENTS

Limousine. Thank you, Ralph and Lisa, for hiring me in my most serious hour of need, training me, and giving me a much-needed boost to my fragile ego.

To my clients whom I drive for quite often—Erin and Wes Jacobs, Melissa and Tony Marcogliese, Gina and Jim Magill, Beth and Wyatt Crowell, Abby and Lloyd Gerry, Charlene and Dan Ryan, Francesca and Michael Breheney, Dana and Casey Brooks, Margot and Ben Fooshee, Kim and Greg Gaynor, Samantha and Bryce O'Brien, Chrissa and John Skeadas, Martha and Mike Riley, Gwen and Bill Guthrie, Stacy and Baret Upham, and Cyndi and Farhood Azima, to name a few—thank you for always trusting me behind the wheel. You gave my life a new start in Bedford, and you helped heal a broken man.

I would like to mention a couple of young girls I drove to their schools, Lana Breheney and Clementine Marcogliese. Your parents always trusted me to drive you safely there. The highest compliment to a driver is when parents trust you with their most precious commodity: their child. And to Carina and Tony Cahan, your conversations and support of Oliver were appreciated. Thank you, Carina, for letting Lucy and Laura drive you to the airport on my most difficult day.

To my friends at the Bedford Free Library, thank you. You let me wander in there when I first moved to Bedford and quietly mill about the library wondering how to jump-start my life again. Ann, Silvia, and Robyn were most patient with me. You gave me a genuine feeling of "community," which I had not felt for a very long time.

Amy and Robert Brault were always in my corner rooting for me to survive. Thank you for being there for me, and your prayers for Oliver's return were heard loud and clear. My friend Larry DelVecchio, we met in 1996 in New Rochelle and have had good times together during our most difficult moments. Thank you being a good friend.

Paul Perea, my friend since fourth grade. You could not be there in New York when this happened, but thank you for your thoughts and prayers.

I'd like to thank the friends who supported my start as a DJ in New York City in 1991: Peter Ferraro, Patrick Browne, Nick Felder, and Martin Canellakis. And of course, Max Jerome (1964-2018), I'll never forget your infectious smile!

Out of pure fear, I could not pick up the phone and talk with anyone in business. That all changed in 1993. Curtis Kleinman hired me to be a recruiter and knocked that fear out of me. He saw something in me greater than I ever could see.

Thank you.

To all my Facebook followers, who provided me with prayers of hope, thank you. Many of you came to the party for Oliver and bestowed him with many gifts, and then again a week later on his birthday! Thank you for sharing my story over and over.

There is a special place in my heart for my neighbors, Bzee and Sherman Durfee. God spared me that long, awful walk up your driveway that dark Sunday. I am so thankful you were not home when Oliver was stolen, only because I know how much you both love him. Thank you for watching him when I get busy. Knowing he is with you two makes me confident to go out and do my work. I love you both for loving my Oliver and taking such good care of him.

I cannot thank all my favorite musical artists, because I would need another chapter for that alone. In my worst of moments, I could always depend on music to save me. I have two artists I must mention, Elvis Presley and Sam Cooke. Thank you for dedicating your lives to your craft. Your God-given talents have always lifted my spirits and given me hope.

Speaking of music, a special thank you to the Equinox Gym in Armonk, New York, for providing such a great environment for me to "dance" to my favorite songs. Your staff is amazing.

I would like to acknowledge my best friends in the world, my dogs: Marcie, Coffee, Mickey, Louie, and Oliver. It was your unconditional love that got me here. What a great gift you dogs are to us humans. You have enriched my life, taught me how to cherish the moment, and most importantly, you have taught me wisdom.

My Oliver, you are loved beyond what words can describe. When I look at you, I am amazed. Amazed you are with me today, amazed that you love me, and amazed at what I learn from you every day. Thank you, Oliver for never giving up on me, because I never gave up on you.

Finally, to you the reader, thank you for letting me share the story of my life and my love of Oliver. I hope this story resonates in your heart as it did mine and gives you understanding that in the darkest of moments you are never alone. Understanding is, indeed, the reward of faith.

About the Authors

Steven J. Carino was born in Huntington, New York. The youngest of five children, he graduated from SUNY Brockport with a bachelor of science in American history. He worked as a DJ in New York City before launching careers in advertising and real estate and starting his own employment agency. Today, Steven has his own driving business and lives in a cottage in Bedford, New York, with his best friend, Oliver, and an array of sheep, goats, chickens, a horse, a rooster, and a miniature cow named Anna Belle. *Oliver* is Steven's first book.

Alex Tresniowski is a former human-interest writer at *People* and the bestselling author of several books, most notably *The Vendetta*, which was purchased by Universal Studios and used as a basis for the movie *Public Enemies*. His other titles include *An Invisible Thread*, *Waking Up in Heaven*, *The Light Between Us*, and his latest book—the true-crime story *The Rope*—will be out in 2021.